Nobody knows how it feels to grow old. I say that because I have asked many people from ages 65 to 93, and they have almost always replied, with a look of bemused astonishment, that they feel just exactly the way they did at 25.

The wonderment with which old people often say, "I feel just the way I felt at 25!" indicates that when they speak of old age, they have in mind something different from the rest of their life. In our imagination old age involves, not merely different challenges, but different creatures—wrinkled, trembly, spotted creatures. We imagine them to be very different from ourselves. Lo and behold, we become them. And they are surprised.

—From *AS OUR YEARS INCREASE*

Also by Tim Stafford,

Knowing the Face of God:
  The Search for a Personal Relationship with God

AS OUR YEARS INCREASE

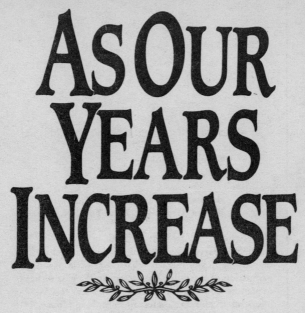

Loving, Caring,
Preparing: A Guide

TIM STAFFORD

HarperPaperbacks
A Division of HarperCollins Publishers

HarperPaperbacks *A Division of* HarperCollins*Publishers*
10 East 53rd Street, New York, N.Y. 10022

This book was originally published in 1989 by Zondervan
Publishing House.

Unless otherwise noted, Scripture quotations are taken
from the *Holy Bible: New International Version* (North
American Edition), copyright © 1973, 1978, 1984 by The
International Bible Society. Used by permission of
Zondervan Bible Publishers.

First HarperPaperbacks printing: January 1991

Printed in the United States of America

HarperPaperbacks and colophon are trademarks of
HarperCollins*Publishers*

10 9 8 7 6 5 4 3 2 1

CONTENTS

ACKNOWLEDGMENTS

I owe a particular debt of thanks to Chris Baird, who did a great deal of the interviewing that formed the foundation of this book. She was an invaluable help, and did outstanding work. She also read the manuscript and made useful suggestions.

A number of people read the manuscript and made helpful comments: Joseph Allison, David and Carol Andersen, Stephen Sheerin, Harold Smith, Popie Stafford, Elizabeth Wrightman, and Philip Yancey. My mother and father, Harriette and Chase Stafford, and my wife's parents, Henry and Ozzie Belle Herrod, read the manuscript, made suggestions, and above all allowed me to use their lives as a reference point. Anne Severance, Bob Hudson, and Nia Jones served as my capable, cheerful editors at Zondervan. Without the help of these friends, this book would be poorer at many points.

There were finally a host of people who allowed themselves to be interviewed, telling freely about their own family experiences. Some of these are referred to by name in this book; the stories of others have been told with names changed to disguise their identities, and some are not referred to simply because not all the stories could be included in a single volume. All, however, contributed to my understanding of aging. Many inspired me and encouraged me by the quality of their lives. The lessons they learned, and the wisdom they shared, I have attempted to pass on.

As Our Years Increase

PROLOGUE

MEMO TO MY FATHER-IN-LAW:

THIS BOOK BEGAN WITH YOU, HENRY, ON A DAY when you asked me how Popie and I intended to take care of you when you got old. Maybe "asked" is the wrong word. To me, it sounded like you demanded to know.

I hadn't given it a serious thought. After all, you were some years away from retirement. I must admit, I disliked your insistence that we answer a hypothetical question—particularly one so unsettling to consider.

You were sure of one thing: you never would enter a nursing home of your own free will. So how did we, living 2,000 miles away, intend to care for you? You asked me or Popie that question repeatedly over a number of years. I never learned to like it any better. But I came to see it as a fair question.

I suppose your experiences as a doctor made you peculiarly aware of old age. Most of us manage to keep older people out of our minds. Those with serious problems are mainly invisible to us: they stay in their homes, in nursing homes, or in hospitals.

1

They don't come to church (though they remain on the church rolls). We don't meet them at work. They conveniently disappear.

But as a doctor you spent much of your life in hospitals and nursing homes. You felt for a feathery pulse in birdlike limbs. You visited withered old men who needed an operation but were not strong enough to have one. You saw people give up and die.

So I imagine. The truth is that, even with your insistent questioning, I have not found it easy to talk about old age—not with you and Ozzie, nor with my own parents. I have felt that you do not find it easy to talk about with me, either. It seems too hypothetical, remote, unlikely—and perhaps too frightening. We know so little about what will come.

This I do know: we will go through it together. We are bound by blood and by love, and that bond will hold us through whatever lies ahead. I say this as a deeply felt certainty. If I have learned anything about old age, I have learned that it is a family time. Even in our pleasure-driven, divorce-and-forget society, children take care of their parents. Popie and I will, as much as it lies in our power.

Much of this book is very practical, nuts-and-bolts information. I have read books and papers, talked to experts, interviewed elderly people and the children of elderly people. I have sifted through reams of material on aging, in order to find the most important "how-to" information. Originally that was all I intended to do, for I felt that your question led simply to practical matters like retirement finances and medical care.

I found myself, however, needing to go on. Could we be satisfied with just this—the management of the gradual disintegration of life? Is it enough to reassure ourselves that the vast majority need never enter a nursing home? Is our chief hope that you die painlessly, while asleep? Or make the most of one last hurrah?

I can't believe any part of life should be so utterly grim. My faith won't allow it. I felt that I had to probe a harder question, one that the vast literature on aging almost entirely ignores: What is aging for? Is there a point to it, and if so, what? If we insist on believing in dignity for all human beings, dignity for Alzheimer's victims, dignity for the poor, dignity for the dying, how may we understand that dignity as anything more than a theoretical sentiment?

I think old age forces such questions on us. So much may be stripped away (though it is not always). What is left? And what is its meaning? And why the stripping in the first place? What is God doing with old people?

I have to ask these questions as I see you nowadays strain to get in and out of a chair. Already you have given up your work. More will be given up, regardless of how well you manage your health. What, if anything, will be gained?

Growing Past 65: How Does It Feel to Grow Old?

NOBODY KNOWS HOW IT FEELS TO GROW OLD. I say that because I have asked many people from ages 65 to 93, and they have almost always replied, with a look of bemused astonishment, that they feel just exactly the way they did at 25.

I remember my grandmother talking about this not long before her death. She was in her seventies, but an almost kittenish quality surfaced. She marveled: How could it be that she had reached this ripe old age without any sense that she had changed from an 18-year-old girl?

At 79, author J.B. Priestley put it this way: "It is as though walking down Shaftesbury Avenue as a fairly young man, I was suddenly kidnapped, rushed into a theater and made to don the gray hair, the wrinkles and the other attributes of age, then wheeled on-stage. Behind the appearance of age I am the same person, with the same thoughts, as when I was younger."

5

Researchers Tuckmann and Lorge asked a sample of Americans how they identified themselves. Of those *over 80*, 53 percent admitted they were old; 36 percent reported that they considered themselves middle-aged, and 11 percent, young. Nearly half, that is, thought of themselves as either young or middle-aged.

You could take this to mean that old people reject and deny their own age. Judging by my conversations, though, a more likely interpretation is that experiences (the mirror, bodily aches and pains, the attitudes of others) gradually convince old people that they are old. To accept this, they must contradict their own internal sense of themselves. They feel as young as ever.

So while legions of researchers compile statistics and multiply information on old age, they mask an amusing and startling reality: the people whom they so diligently study feel like impostors. In truth, the old themselves ask (and keep on asking, and looking around them in hopes of discovering) what it is like to be old.

The wonderment with which old people often say, "I feel just the way I felt at 25!" indicates that when they speak of old age, they have in mind something different from the rest of their life. In our imagination old age involves, not merely different challenges, but different *creatures*—wrinkled, trembly, spotted creatures. We imagine them to be very different from ourselves. Lo and behold, we become them. And we are surprised.

The man, 76 years old, was clearly out of his head. He had been moved to the nursing home directly from the hospital, where he had experienced acute heart failure. Within a few days, however, he seemed better. The trouble was, he kept insisting that his mother would drive over to pick him up. The nurses, who see a good deal of mental confusion, assured him that he would be all right. Privately they decided to keep him for a few more weeks, to see whether his mental state would improve. Eventually, however, his 95-year-old mother, accompanied by her 97-year-old sister, did arrive in her car to take her little boy to his home 100 miles away.

As told in Morton Puner's
To the Good, Long Life.

Our Changing Situation

We need an unclouded look at what old age really is. Often our mental images obscure the truth. In this first chapter, I want to concentrate on questioning preconceptions and introducing facts that will help us to better define old age and its value.

Mankind has never before faced a situation quite like the one confronting us today. Some men and women have always lived to a ripe old age, but they have been a tiny minority. Nowadays, the majority who reach 65 can expect to live into their eighties. They can plan on fifteen to twenty years—nearly one-third of adult life—with most of those years spent in good health.

In times past, such a long life was exceptional. The local newspaper sent out reporters to ask, half seriously, for the secret of an oldster's longevity. Religious people had an answer: They viewed old age as a sign of God's favor. The Book of Proverbs tells us,

> Gray hair is a crown of splendor;
>   it is attained by a righteous life (16:31).

Few would think to say that now. Most people achieve gray hair. The newspaper sends no reporters. The question currently asked is not, "What is the secret of your longevity?" but "Do you want to be kept alive?" What was once a sign of God's blessing has become the source of troubled questions about euthanasia.

Three changes have created the new situation. First, and obviously, more people survive to the limits of life. Medicine has now extended the outer limits. A few people have lived to be 100 throughout recorded history. But in turn-of-the-century America, not one person out of 25 reached 65. Now almost everybody does.

Not only do they survive, but they are in better health. Few people who are 65 are truly "old" any more. Most are still vigorous. But (and this is the second change) in 1934 the Social Security Administration froze the age of retirement at 65. Sixty-five was decreed "old"—and even though people live considerably longer now, 65 has remained "old."

Many are strong enough to continue working. But given the choice, few do. The age of retirement has, in fact, dipped; currently it is, on average, 63. Somewhat artificially, we have created an extended period of "no responsibilities" by ending a person's working life at 65. If a person wishes to work beyond that point, it is possible, but Social Security regulations make it financially disadvantageous. For the first time in history, we have a huge group of people with no working responsibilities.

The third change is the increased ability of doctors to keep people alive when they are in terrible health. Nobody who enters a nursing home can miss seeing how many live a shadowy half-life there, not quite sick enough to die but too sick to know their own family and friends. It is true that only 5 percent of people over 65 can be found in a nursing home at any given time. But for those reaching the age of 85, the percentage is 23. According to a 1984 report published by the Federal Council on Aging: "In the last two decades, drops in cardiac mortality alone have added several years to life expectancy. Yet the truly significant impact of this revolution has not been in keeping the healthy alive. On the contrary, the extension of life expectancy for the ill and disabled has been the truly extraordinary impact of the gerontological revolution."

Just forty years ago many of these people would have died of pneumonia, the "old man's friend." Twenty years ago they would have died of heart failure. Now they can be steered through a crisis, but they remain too frail to recover fully. The odds are in our favor, as individuals, that we will not experience such an ending. But since we all have two parents, and most of us have two parents-in-law, the odds are that we *will* carry some responsibility for a parent who is quite dependent. The "frail elderly," or the "old old," as those over 85 are called, are the fastest-growing group in our society, predicted to increase 64 percent by the year 2000, and to triple between 1980 and 2030.

Breaking Out of Silence

Your likelihood of becoming one of those "wrinkled, spotted creatures," therefore, has greatly increased. Those whose image of old age is negative—who find old age a depressing subject—are bound to find the world increasingly dismal.

The best antidote for that attitude is to talk with older people. Much fear of old age comes from superficial contact. You see an old lady struggling painfully down the hallway, using her cane, and think how terrible such difficulty must be. Or, while singing Christmas carols at a nursing home, you catch glimpses of serious, maybe terminal, illness.

Sit down to talk with that old lady, or spend an afternoon

in that nursing home, and you may well come away with a different perspective. Most elders are happy—or at least are happy on the majority of days. Most are thoughtful and brave about their condition—each in his own way. They are not a faceless mass. They are individuals who bring a lifetime of resourcefulness to their difficulties.

Even in the grimmest circumstances you discover moving signs of grace. As Elizabeth Wrightman notes, "Nobody who has spent much time in a nursing home can escape the sense of a community of caring people often found there, the volunteers, the many little moments filled with hope and intimacy, the staff who are often particularly fond of the elderly."

But this positive picture of aging is seldom seen. Most people, until they are older themselves, know few if any older people well.

There is one great exception—in families. When I first began research for this book, I expected to look high and low for families who had had illuminating experiences in caring for aging parents. I soon found that very little searching was necessary. I had only to mention the subject, and almost invariably some remarkable drama would be revealed. Someone would remember growing up sharing a bedroom with Grandpa. Someone else would tell me about caring for a mother with Alzheimer's disease. A friend would describe the frustration she was experiencing in trying to find a living situation for her parents. The stories came from people I knew, yet in most cases their situations were news to me. They, I further discovered, generally knew very little about what *their* friends had gone through. They made choices, sometimes very difficult and sudden choices, without much idea of what to do or whom to ask.

Ask for yourself—ask almost anybody—and you will

hear, time after time, a moving story of family solidarity. But people don't normally talk about it. If someone in the family had cancer, or was caring for a child with neurological damage, their neighbors and friends and fellow church members would know. Yet people outside the family know next to nothing about Grandma. They aren't asked to pray for her. They aren't asked to help out. "She's doing as well as could be expected," the family members say, and let it go at that. Maybe they do so because they don't expect much from Grandma—they think her life is over. Maybe they are silent because her condition reminds them of the inevitability of their own old age.

Public Hope, Private Nightmare

Out of our society's silence about old age, we fasten on two very strong, contradictory images. One is the horror of horrors: a body strapped to a bed—full of tubes, mind gone—kept alive by machines. We fear that image, for ourselves or for our loved ones.

Our alternative image is a sunny, mellow grandparent, dithering in the garden or reading stories to a grandchild. This is an image of peace, an end to aggressiveness, an acceptance of life.

In conversation, we try to dwell on the sunny grandparent figure. The closest we usually get to articulating our fears is to say, "I hope I die in my sleep." But beneath our hopeful cheer, undermining it, is our private nightmare of the body strapped to the bed. This terrifying image keeps us from talking or even thinking about aging.

When Paul Tournier was reading various books on this subject, his wife asked him to "at least leave the books face down on the table" because their rather funereal titles were so depressing. Why depressing? Because for us (though not for all people of all times), the mere mention of aging brings unpleasant pictures to mind.

Neither the body-in-the-bed image nor the sunny-grandparent image does justice to the experience of aging. The years between 65 and 90 are probably the most dynamic period of life, excepting childhood.

When I think back to the first twenty years of my own life, I see many different pictures. I see myself in the bath, grinning in naked splendor. I see myself standing, perhaps at the age of four, in our winter-bound front yard, dressed in an awkward wool coat. I see my open, trusting expression as I hold a crayon in a pose for first-grade photos. I see myself as a distant, awkward teenager, tall enough to stand in the back of family photos. When I see these pictures, I remember the way I felt in each stage: secure, exhilarated, frightened, confused. Each time had a mentality of its own.

Think back to the stages you passed through in your first twenty years. It would be impossible to capture all those years in a single image—a picture of a newborn baby, of a toddler having a tantrum, of a Little Leaguer at bat, of two adolescents holding hands on a ski slope. You would need a whole photo album to picture the first twenty years of life, for childhood is continuous and turbulent change.

So is old age. The last twenty years of life bring nearly as many changes as the first twenty. Yet in that storm of change, there is continuity—the character of the individual.

My grandfather would seem to exemplify in himself the two contradictory images of old age, since he passed from one to the other in a matter of days.

While in his seventies, he visited my aunt and her family in Pakistan, where they were missionaries. As a young man he had traveled Pakistan (then part of India) by camel, and later by Model T, going from village to village to speak of Jesus Christ. He had always been a vigorous person, of strong opinions and memorable determination, ever ready with a joke and a pocketful of candy should he encounter any children. In Pakistan he had spent most of his life. In Pakistan his children had been born.

Now he was having a grand time, visiting old places and playing with his grandchildren. In the lakes of Kashmir he tried waterskiing for the first time in his life.

While there he had a stroke. He spent weeks in a little mission hospital, and when his condition stabilized, it became clear that the stroke had destroyed those portions of his brain dealing with communication. We learned that the problem had a name: aphasia. Aphasia left his intelligence intact; it only took away his ability to speak and write, to read, and to understand speech. For some time he was convinced, in his native stubbornness, that it was *the world's* problem, not his. Why wouldn't people speak clearly?

Since my grandmother had died the year before, Grandpa came home to live alone in a little house near ours. For a time he took speech therapy and read sentences into a cassette tape recorder for as many as eight hours at a time. Eventually, failing to see any progress, he quit. He watched television some of the time. He was a man who had read voluminously, and he could no longer read. He still wrote letters, but they were a pastiche of unrecognizable words and phrases. When he spoke, his words came out gibberish, though you could tell by his insistent attempts that he had a very specific meaning in mind. It was as though a crazed electrician had gone into his brain and rewired the connections.

So he spent the last ten years of his life with his thoughts. He would come to my parents' home for special occasions—for Christmas Day, or Thanksgiving, or when one of his grown grandchildren came home. His face always wore a jovial expression. He would hold a baby or play with a small child, and sometimes he would still try to talk. With the occasional word that came out right, and a combination of intonation and body language, we could understand most things if we worked long and hard at it. Sometimes, unmistakably, he would try to ask my father (a theological peer) about the meaning of suffering. But inevitably the effort to communicate was too great. He would tire and give up. The frustration showed plainly on his ruddy face. Sometimes he would cry, this man who had never cried. He would find a chair and doze into sleep. Among those he loved best in the world, he was alone.

As the years passed—long years—his health failed gradually. His articulation slackened, and his sounds became more repetitive, like those of a child who has yet to learn speech. He retained his remarkable, energetic, hopeful face. But as he lost control of his sphincter muscles, he often smelled of urine. He went into a nursing home. He drooled. He shuffled. Now stooped, he seemed shorter.

He wanted to die; he said so, urgently enough so that we understood. He prayed to die. One day he announced to my mother—it is strange, but somehow they could communicate—that he was going to die. He held out his arms and in his deep, patriarch's voice pronounced final blessing on her. He then dismissed her and, lying down on his bed, folded his hands on his chest. He closed his eyes.

About half an hour later he realized that this was not his day to die. He got up, quite angry. He had always given orders with the expectation that they would be obeyed. But he could not order his death.

I still felt, when I saw him, that a kind of greatness showed through. He barely came up to my chin, but he was a very big man to me. I knew what was inside him. But that greatness gradually clouded over until God answered his prayers.

Altering the Images

Superficially, my grandfather's old age was neatly divided into our public hope and our private nightmare: all that is best and worst in old age. Waterskiing one day, drooling the next.

I do have those two kinds of memories—his strong, crinkled smile and Scottish burr before the stroke and his depressed, withdrawn expression after the stroke. But in my memory I cannot convincingly break his life into two parts: one good and the other bad. There is one man in the middle of both. If anything, I think of his hard years as the richest. In his suffering, he showed us the stuff he was made of. I would never wish such torment on anybody, but I am grateful I witnessed my grandfather passing through it.

The two extreme images of old age rarely hold up when considering a specific individual. Yet they are persistent, powerful images, probably because they both deal, in separate ways, with our fears of old age.

The sunny grandparent image deals with fears by denying their reality. A woman who conducts seminars on aging told me that the first response to her introductory session usually includes something like this: "My grandmother is 92, and she doesn't act a bit old. Last summer she climbed a mountain, and we could hardly keep up with her!" or "Longevity runs in our family. My great uncle lived to be 89. I'm planning on being just like him!"

Naturally we admire seniors who stay vital, who are full of energy and good health. Most elders fit that description, even into their eighties or nineties. But the admiration can be used, unconsciously, to distance ourselves from the fearsome realities of aging. Focusing solely on the image of the sunny grandparent suggests that old age need not be difficult. People almost hint that elders who are not active and vibrant are somehow to blame for their condition. They ought to "think young"!

Though the majority of elders never become disabled, every aging person lives under the immediate threat of disability, degeneration, and loss. A realistic view of aging stares that possibility squarely in the face.

We Need New Values

Yet a realistic view of aging is not overwhelmed by fear either. It finds value in every stage of life, including old age.

In former ages, elders were society's link to the accumulated wisdom of their ancestors. Elders knew when to plant seeds, how to preserve food. They knew the old legends. With a lifetime of experience, elders knew what to do in a crisis; this could make the difference between survival and decimation. But in modern industrial societies, wisdom is found in the library, and among the youngish, recently educated experts who are constantly putting new volumes into those libraries. The old have little to do with this modern form of wisdom; and they have lost other ways of proving themselves useful. They seldom work, and they are no longer fashionably beautiful or desirable. We have more old people than ever before in America, and their population is growing at a faster rate than the population of India. Yet we don't know what they are good for. Even old people don't know what they are supposed to do, except to relax and enjoy the "sunset years," or to build their defenses against the helplessness they fear is coming.

When children think of their parents' old age, their typical concerns are defensive: Will I have to put Mother into a nursing home? Will we run out of money? Can we spare our parents from suffering?

The great concerns of the elderly are a mirror image of these: Please, God, may I not be a burden to my children. Save me from the nursing home. Let me keep my faculties. Take me quietly and quickly when it's my time to go.

Both children and elders are apprehensive about old age. Their fears are realistic, to a certain extent. But surely twenty years cannot be lived in a purely defensive way. Is there no more positive purpose to old age?

Think about the average reaction to a church that is mainly made up of older people. Pastors "stuck" in such a church often feel helpless to accomplish anything. "I look out from the pulpit and see nothing but gray!" they complain. Even the older people in the church feel "stuck." "We've got to bring in some young families, or this church will die." They speak as though the elderly had ceased to exist, as though they no longer counted.

We need a better image of old age—one that faces hardship, but is not overwhelmed by fear. For that, we need a sense of the good things God intends in old age. Unfortunately, much of the folk wisdom we have inherited offers just the opposite—sheer pessimism.

One of Grimm's fairy tales goes this way: God had set 30 years as the span of life for all animals, including man. The ass, the dog and the monkey thought it too long, however, and begged God to reduce their years by 18, 12 and 10. The man, however, was greedy. He asked to be given these extra years, and God agreed. So man's years totaled 70.

The first 30 are his own, and they pass quickly. The next 18 are the ass's, and during these he has to carry countless burdens on his back. Then come the dog's 12, when he can do little but growl and drag himself from one corner to another, for he has no teeth left. After these are over, man is left with the monkey's 10. He is no longer in his right mind, but grows rather strange, doing things that make children laugh at him.

The Encouraging Heritage of Scripture

As Grimm's story demonstrates, the fear of aging has a long history. We are heirs of an ancient tradition that stereotypes and stigmatizes old age—the wicked old witch, the lecherous old man. It is not merely a popular tradition, either; great philosophers such as Aristotle have written extensively of the "disgusting degeneration of the old."

The Bible offers a very different heritage. Old age is consistently a blessing, a gift from God. It is valued not merely by the elderly themselves, but by the whole community. Old Testament law commands everyone to rise in the presence of the aged (Lev. 19:32). When Job's theologian-friends sat down with him to debate God's justice in ruining Job's life, their conversation assumed that elders normally had the edge in sorting out difficult questions (Job 12:20; 15:10; 32:7). You respect such people, unless you are perverse. The commandment to honor parents (Exod. 20:12) is a specific application of the wider expectation that you honor your elders.

Does the Bible idealize old age? Hardly. Isaac (Gen. 27:1), Jacob (48:10), Eli (1 Sam. 3:2) and Ahijah (1 Kings 14:4) all suffered from failing eyesight; Barzillai (2 Sam. 19:35) was hard of hearing and lost his sense of taste, and David had chronically poor circulation in his last years (1 Kings 1:1–4). These cases are presented as facts that require no explanation.

The author of Ecclesiastes, predictably, gave the most graphic view of aging:

Remember your Creator in the days of your youth,
before the days of trouble come and the years approach when
  you will say,
"I find no pleasure in them"—
before the sun and the light and the moon and the stars
  grow dark,
and the clouds return after the rain;
when the keepers of the house tremble [hands],
and the strong men stoop [legs],
when the grinders cease because they are few [teeth],
and those looking through the windows grow dim [eyes];
when the doors to the street are closed [isolation]
and the sound of grinding fades [loss of strength, work];
when men rise up at the sound of birds [insomnia],
but all their songs grow faint [hearing];
when men are afraid of heights
and of dangers in the streets [fear];
when the almond tree blossoms [white hair]
and the grasshopper drags himself along [ungainly walk]
and desire no longer is stirred [impotence].
Then man goes to his eternal home
and mourners go about the streets [death].

Ecclesiastes 12:1–5

With such a frank view of old age, it is remarkable that
anyone would wish to experience it. Yet for the Old Testament Jew, long life was one of the prime benefits of godly
living. (See, for example, Abraham's blessing in Genesis
15:15.) There is no prayer in the Bible pleading to avoid
its difficulties, no request for eternal youth. What the author
of Psalm 71 does pray for is God's saving presence through
the time of trial: "Do not cast me away when I am old; do
not forsake me when my strength is gone. . . . Even when
I am old and gray, do not forsake me, O God. . . ." Another
psalm seems to answer this plea, expressing the assurance
of God's care, acquired through decades of experience: "I
was young and now I am old, yet I have never seen the

righteous forsaken or their children begging bread" (37:25).

They loved life; they saw all of it, even the hard parts, as a gift. Life came from the very breath of God forming and animating the dust; it required no justification, only thankfulness. The Hebrews feared death, but not in an exaggerated, terrified way. Death was an end they knew they must encounter one day. Yet they had confidence that God could and would sustain them; therefore, they could face severe difficulties without panic. "If God be for me, who can be against me?" So they seemed to view any struggle. And so they loved long lives.

Perhaps this love is revealed most clearly by the prophets, who portrayed the renewed world God would recreate. They foresaw an earth in which spears will be made into plowshares and lions will lie down with lambs. According to Isaiah, "Never again will there be in it . . . an old man who does not live out his years; he who dies at a hundred will be thought a mere youth. . . ." (65:20). And Zechariah paints this lovely portrait: " 'Once again men and women of ripe old age will sit in the streets of Jerusalem, each with a cane in hand because of his age. The city streets will be filled with boys and girls playing there' " (8:4,5).

Death, Old Testament prophecies suggest, will be destroyed in the end. But old age—unsteady enough to need a cane, yet free enough at heart to share the street with children—is a part of the portrait of a beautiful new world.

Their love of life, nonetheless, did not keep Old Testament believers from knowing its grief. "The length of our days is seventy years—or eighty, if we have the strength; yet their span is but trouble and sorrow, for they quickly pass, and we fly away. . . . Teach us to number our days aright, that we may gain a heart of wisdom" (Ps. 90:10, 12).

What does it mean to "number our days"? Moses, to

whom this deep, austere psalm was credited, spent decades as a shepherd. A shepherd's use of mathematics is rudimentary: he counts his sheep to ensure that none goes missing. Unless he counts, and counts carefully, he cannot be sure that he has kept his sheep well. So we are to number our days in this long, brief life, to ensure that none goes missing—that we do not squander the gift of God, through carelessness letting days or weeks or years slip away unnoticed, without profit.

That, it seems to me, is just what many people nowadays would like to do with old age: to let it slip away unnoticed. The Psalmist's view is different. The fundamental mathematics of "numbering our days" is that old age is good, good even if hard. It is good because it is part of life as God made it. It is good because God is in it. Not a day should be missed.

The Seven Days of Old Age

I am an optimist about old age. I think a Christian is compelled to be. It is not enough, however, to call aging "good" in vaguely optimistic terms. We need to be specific. We will need to look realistically at what getting old involves at each stage. Then we can ask what is good about it.

For the purposes of simple classification, gerontologists often break old age into three parts: the "young old" from 65 to 74, the "middle old" from 75 to 84, and the "frail elderly" or "old old" from 85 up. If you meet a handsome, silver-haired couple on their way to Australia, eager to lie on the beach, you can regard them as among the young old. A woman in a nursing home, immobile and unable to carry on a conversation, is probably among the "old old."

However, all such age classifications are necessarily inexact. Some young people develop Alzheimer's disease, and some much older people travel and enjoy the beach. Change is sometimes gradual and sometimes catastrophic; it may affect one part of the person's life and not another; and of course, people respond very differently to the changes they are dealt. One could make a case for dozens of classifications—or for no classifications at all.

The years beyond 65 cannot be summed up in one image, or three stages, but require a whole album of pictures. I have chosen seven of these pictures—the most important ones, I believe—and identified them as "seven days." We will examine this "week of old age" through the remainder of this book. In each day, we will look for the good in God's purposes.

A week suggests both the variety and the continuity of old age. Each day in the week is different, yet the tasks of one day tend to set the stage for the next. Also, a week has a definite direction. It ends with the Sabbath—the blessed day of rest and worship.

- **The First Day**—the Freedom Day—begins with retirement, which introduces the life of leisure. The great challenge is to make good use of freedom, to deal responsibly with a life "without responsibilities." Having finished their career, elders must find their vocation.
- **The Second Day**—the Day of Reflection—leads an elder to begin meditating on his life. Often a sudden shock—perhaps a mild stroke, or the death of a near friend—precipitates a mental readjustment. The Second Day is less busy, increasingly meditative.
- **The Third Day**—the Widow's Day—comes with the loss of a spouse. For the one left behind, there is tremendous loneliness and grief, but also the requirement and opportunity to form a new self-definition.
- **The Fourth Day**—the Role-Reversal Day—begins when an

older person needs regular help to get along. She must deal with her own dependency, and if her children are involved in helping, with being parented by those she has parented. Relationships must be renegotiated. On this day, particularly, we are forced to look for the good in losses.

- **The Fifth Day**—the Dependence Day—comes when a person must lean on others for basic life maintenance—eating, bathing, dressing. Often the whole family is involved at this stage, and must make critical decisions about who will provide this care, and how. There is a need to foster dignity and purpose, even in the face of grave disability.
- **The Sixth Day**—the Farewell Day—is the period preparing for death.
- **The Seventh Day**—the Sabbath Day—is the day of worship, the day of rest. While a secularist must see death as the end, Christians see it as the beginning of a new life. For families left behind, the Seventh Day is a period for recapturing the whole image of the person who has died.

Parents and Children Together

How can we gain a view of old age that is positive, honorable, hopeful? Some of it comes just with looking at the facts. God loves older people, and he has created them with inherent dignity.

But another side of the dignity and worth of old age comes more specifically from a Christian understanding of the world. I don't know how materialists can see good in some aspects of old age; I would think they would be forced toward euthanasia. Christians, however, understand the existence of another world, the world of God's love, toward which or against which our lives are being shaped. If you believe in this other world, it is not very hard to see that old age is meant to prepare us for it. So much that will be valueless there becomes, already, valueless here—independence, pride, wealth. So much that the kingdom of love depends on becomes already vitally necessary—interdependence, kindness, humility.

These qualities are usually expressed in families. To a remarkable degree, children and other relatives do get involved. While other relationships may shrivel to almost nothing, family relationships often grow stronger. They certainly grow more intense. Because of this, I will avoid taking sides—just the view of elders, or just the view of their children. Both elders and their children are involved, so I am writing to both.

In that interlocking of parents and children, part of the goodness of the hardness of old age reveals itself. You see the solidarity of human beings of all ages, a solidarity expressed concretely by the family. We really are in this together, from birth to death. Though this togetherness is sometimes extremely wearing, it is fundamentally good. It is good that we learn to bear each other's burdens—that the young care for the old, and the old for the young, according to their different capacities. If we really could be forever young, due to megavitamins or magic, this intergenerational care might never occur.

DAY 1

❧

MEMO TO MY FATHER:

POPIE'S FATHER, AS YOU KNOW, HAS MADE THE *final break. He has announced, with quiet finality, that he will close down his office this May. Until he dies people will continue to call him "Dr. Herrod." But the doctor will do no more doctoring.*

The big decision started several years ago, when Henry's heart acted up and he had to quit surgery. After that, his career seemed all but dead to him. Merely to see patients in the office and refer them to other surgeons made him feel like a ball player who, after years at shortstop, takes a job shuffling paper in the club office.

Henry could have gone on for a few more years, peppering patients with pills and advice—poor substitutes, to a surgeon, for cutting them open to fix the trouble. He has decided not to settle for that option. Within a few weeks he will, according to the script, wake up in the morning without an office to go to.

I mention this because I am trying, without much success, to imagine you in the same condition. The way Henry felt about surgery, you feel about preaching. Any other activity is, for you, a poor substitute for that cut and thrust of words, with its promise of changing the world through the Word's surgery on the heart.

Yet you are now, after forty years as a pastor, an "interim." I've taken great pleasure from your pleasure, as this church in Homewood has welcomed you, honored you, appreciated you. Their warmth toward you and Mom has seemed to quiet your restlessness. Your energy is directed outward, into others' lives. Yet this period will be brief—two years, probably, perhaps three, before you must leave and allow a younger minister to carry on.

Interim—the word suggests a holding operation—"until something substantial can begin again." The end of your time was in sight from your first day, which doesn't, I think, bother you terribly. Maybe it would have at one time, when your interest lay more in putting up buildings and organizing young churches. Now, I think, your interest in the dynamics of institutions has dwindled. You have narrowed your concerns to the dynamics of individuals. And to preaching.

Maybe, just maybe, you will go on preaching until you drop. You have certainly not lost a bit of skill. However, as we both know, preaching is a power position normally held by the senior pastor. I don't see you carrying that load much longer. I don't see your interest continuing, let alone your energy. Already, you are happily an interim.

Most likely, when you cease being a senior pastor, you will cease regular preaching. Then you too will truly wake up without an office to go to. What will you do with yourself, when the activity that defines your life is no longer possible? What thoughts will train through your mind when you rise on a dreary morning and find yourself quite free, but not free to spend your energy on the one thing you have lived for?

I picture you getting up, making your ritual cup of coffee, devouring your newspapers, and then, in your normal restlessness, finding no center to the week ahead—nothing to prepare for, to think toward, to anticipate—no Sunday morning.

The First Day:
Freedom

LORRAINE AND HANK HAD A VERY CLEAR GOAL in mind for their retirement: independence. They had two married daughters whom they loved, and grandchildren whom they enjoyed visiting. But living close to those families was not part of their retirement plan. Early in their married life Lorraine's mother had lived with them through a long illness. Hank and Lorraine both retained unpleasant memories of that experience, which made them determined not to burden their own children. Besides, after forty years tied to Hank's demanding career in sales, they wanted to make their plans without consulting a soul. Lorraine and Hank had their own life to live.

So they were shocked when, shortly before retirement, they toured their younger daughter's new home, then under construction. Their daughter indicated, with pride, a small separate apartment.

29

"You're not building us a place to retire, are you?" Hank asked.

"Of course we are," his daughter replied. "What else are you going to do? We want you to come and live with us."

Hank and Lorraine were astonished. They thought they had made their intentions perfectly clear. "We had always been very open," Lorraine says. "We were going to find a good place to retire, and we were going to do what we wanted without ever asking, 'May I?' Our mouths were hanging open, and their mouths were hanging open. I guess they felt we had just pulled the rug out from under them."

To the distress of their daughter, Hank and Lorraine settled in a retirement complex that provided the full range of medical care and assistance. Though some distance from their children, they visit often. They consider their choice of the retirement complex "one of the smartest decisions we've ever made." They feel stimulated and supported by retired people who live around them, and they derive peace of mind from their independence. "When I had my two surgeries," Lorraine reports happily, "it was no concern of my children. They knew I would have whatever good care I needed. Nobody felt compelled to come to see that I got along all right, or that Hank did what he was supposed to do. I was no burden for anybody!"

Retirement: It Usually Feels Wonderful

Retirement begins the changes. It brings the first great loss—of career—and introduces a new leisure society—one marked by golf carts, Winnebagos and retirement communities, to name the more obvious emblems.

Retirement is the change with which the children of seniors can most easily identify, because it is closest to their experience. They easily imagine themselves losing a job—indeed, that is a standard nightmare of middle age—and they also easily imagine the pleasure of a permanent vacation, since they look forward to a few weeks off each year. Younger people find it much harder to empathize with other, later losses—the loss of vision or hearing, for instance—since such physical failures seem distant and remote.

Yet younger people often imagine the First Day quite differently from the way it feels to their parents. Hank and Lorraine's clash with their children is extreme, but their differing expectations are common. While children often expect their parents to become suddenly more dependent—with all that implies, both good and bad—the parents are frequently determined to maintain their independence at all costs. The children may expect unlimited babysitting, while the parents anticipate long trips to the Orient. The children may think of their parents as suddenly old, while the parents think of themselves as suddenly free.

People who have not yet retired often believe that behind the pleasant façade of retirement is a dreadful vacancy. A set of "truths" has been developed to support this view, forming a negative stereotype of aging. A 1975 Harris survey found that younger people overwhelmingly thought older people struggled with sickness, loneliness, feelings of uselessness, and fear of death.

But most older people, responding to the same questions, reported feeling healthy, happy, useful and unafraid. Though happiness is hard to measure, the "young old" years seem to be among the happiest of a person's entire life.

Why shouldn't they be? First, the shadow of death is far away. Life expectancy at 65 is now 15 years for men, 19 years for women, and rising all the time. Not only that, people are retiring younger—most before they reach 65. While as recently as 1955 more than one of four men over 70 were still employed; by 1980 the figure had dropped to 13 percent. Some were forced out or laid off, but far more chose to retire. "We are experiencing something that, on a mass scale, is new in human history: a long period of time in the typical life course beyond the stages of work and family responsibilities," wrote Stephen Crystal in *America's Old Age Crisis.*

At retirement, a senior can anticipate at least ten years of good health—and probably considerably more. According to sociologist Robert Atchley, studies show that "Retired people are no more likely to be sick than people their same age who are still on the job." That generalization actually suggests that the health of retirees tends to *improve,* since some retire because of health problems. Only about 15 percent of all Americans over 65 are unable to carry on "normal activities." The average number of sick days in bed for all elderly is a mere fifteen per year.

Obviously, there are different ways to define good health. A person healthy enough to get out of bed and even onto the golf course may not feel well enough to function at a high-pressure job. My father-in-law is a classic example. He's certainly not bedridden. He's taken numerous pleasure trips in the past year, and expects to take more. He could, undoubtedly, keep up his medical practice. But he does have some serious health concerns, and he does find it much more tiring to do his work. He doesn't feel up to surgery, his real love, at all. Is he in good health or bad health? Bad health, perhaps, if he wants to continue to work at the old pace; good health if he is content to take it easy.

Sound Finances

Not only are the retired in relatively good health, they're in relatively good financial shape, too. The economic status of the elderly has been virtually reversed since the 1950s, when they were among America's most poverty-stricken people. Thanks to Social Security, Medicare and pension plans (which began in the '40s and '50s after the government offered large corporate tax breaks), the elderly are by some measures the most financially stable group in America. If you include as income such government services as Medicare payments, they have a poverty rate of merely 3 percent at this writing. Excluding such services, the poverty line reaches 15 percent, but that's still one of the lowest rates in any age group. The elderly also have far more disposable income to spend on travel and entertainment than any other age group, including those in their twenties and thirties. Never, perhaps, has government so changed the financial status of such a large number of people.

I don't want to exaggerate this picture. Many elderly people remain poor, with little chance of escaping their poverty through the traditional route of ambition and hard work. Single women are particularly susceptible. So are members of minority groups.

But poverty is not the norm. Most older people have some money to spend—especially the "young old" who have recently retired. Most own their own homes without a mortgage. They have roots in a community, and they intend to maintain them. Some do move toward the Sunbelt, but the idea that older people generally flock to warmer climates is a myth. Most stay put.

The elderly are the best educated in history. Between

1960 and 1970 the percentage of those over 65 who had finished high school and college doubled; the percentage has continued to zoom upward ever since. Education, with its emphasis on broadening interests and sharpening abilities, puts retired people in a better position to enjoy their retirement.

So why shouldn't they enjoy it? They have, as a group, good health, predictable finances, and lots of leisure time. It sounds like the good life.

But this should not, emphatically, suggest that retirement is a piece of cake. It is a major transition, as great in its impact as leaving home for the first time, as marriage, as having children. If you think back to big transitions in your own life, there's a good chance the memories are strongly positive. But for some, the memories are of disaster. In all great transitions there is trauma, with some casualties along the way. Retirement is no exception.

Those who enter retirement with a supportive network of friends and family, a strong sense of themselves, a deep spiritual life, wide interests and a flexible style, will probably enjoy retirement immensely. However, those who retire with inadequate finances, poor health, a sick or dying spouse, or poor mental and spiritual resources may lack the resources to cope with this new phase of life.

The Children's Involvement

Since this is a book for families, the question arises: How much should adult children be involved with their parents' retirement? The answer: Not much. It is inappropriate for children to try to impose their own ideas on their parents' retirement plans. These can be discussed if the parents are willing—and usually they are, for they often spend months or years pondering what they will do with their new liberty. But it is not helpful for children to behave as though their parents have suddenly fallen into dependency and need to be cared for. Hank and Lorraine's children were not wrong to offer their home as a place for retirement, only in assuming that Hank and Lorraine would want to live with them. A good all-round test is, "Would I want my parents to do this for me?" Few children would enjoy being surprised by their parents with a building plan that assumes they will move in together.

Children can be involved in at least one area—planning a retirement celebration. We like to mark transitions with ceremony. Weddings, graduations, baptisms, farewell banquets and funerals are all contrived events that allow people to catch up with themselves, to stand for a moment between what has gone before and the new things yet to come. Retirement celebrations do that too.

In the best cases the employer hosts a farewell dinner and offers a token gift. Some bashful testimonies are made. A scrapbook is presented. The dinner may be a small affair, but it offers the retiring person a chance to turn the corner toward a new life.

I daresay, however, that the people honored with such ceremonies are almost always those who need a ceremony least. Farewell dinners are given, generally, for well-liked, well-adjusted men who have enjoyed successful careers. Working women (half are unmarried at retirement, and particularly vulnerable to poverty) are rarely recognized in this way, nor are people who are sick, laid off, or hold low-paying jobs. In addition, women who have worked at home (and often have a harder time becoming accustomed to their husbands' retirement than their husbands) are almost never considered for such a celebration.

Children like Hank's and Lorraine's may be able to do very little for their parents during this period of their lives, but at least they can see that the transition into retirement does not go unmarked. If a dinner is impractical, a 65th birthday party or 40th anniversary may serve the purpose. Failing a gathering, "testimonials" from friends and colleagues can be written and collected in scrapbook form. Or a plaque can be made up and presented to the honoree:

IN RECOGNITION
of forty years of loving service
to the Stafford family
"We never could have made it without you."

Such events are markers beside the path, showing the distance that has been covered and what yet remains to be traveled. Markers, to be effective, should not blend into the landscape. If a ceremony seems self-conscious and embarrassing at the moment, that may make it all the more memorable. Even families who find ceremonies somewhat awkward should make an effort to celebrate the transition to retirement.

Four Critical Concerns

After the celebration, children can best lean back and watch their parents enjoy their new freedom. Children *should*, however, be alert for possible difficulties their parents might face in making the transition. Some critical concerns to watch for are: (1) early adjustments; (2) financial anxiety; (3) marital difficulties; and (4) depression.

1. *Early adjustments.* Many people feel considerable anxiety in the period leading up to their retirement. They may have

heard horror stories from those unprepared for a new life-style. At this early stage, the new retirees simply need reassurance.

Not only do the overwhelming majority enjoy retire-ment—about 85 percent do—but they tend to like it more as they grow used to it. Often they are surprised at how positive the experience is. In one survey of teachers and telephone workers, about 20 percent of those who said they were enjoying retirement reported that they had not an-ticipated they would like it.

Still, adjustments have to be made. Robert Atchley puts retirement into five stages: honeymoon, disenchantment, reorientation, stability and termination. What he says, in a nutshell, is that most people start out thinking retirement is wonderful. They have time to do all the things they never had time to do before—read, garden, travel, fish, loaf. After this honeymoon period, they gradually grow bored and frustrated with these activities. They must come to terms with a new life, not merely the leisure slice of the old one. Eventually most people do reorient themselves and achieve reasonably happy stability, which lasts until they become seriously ill and die (termination).

It is easy for busy younger people to pay closest attention to their parents during the first months of retirement. Dis-covering their elders to be in a "honeymoon" stage, the children will be likely to thank God and move on to other concerns. But the really difficult adjustments, requiring creativity and initiative, may come months or even years later, after the honeymoon is over. During the disenchant-ment and reorientation stages, children should be especially alert. At no point should they barge in and try to make decisions for their parents, but they may listen, encourage, and give a gentle push toward new involvements.

It must be said that a minority of elders completely reject retirement. By one count, about half of all farmers fail to make a satisfactory adjustment. Teachers have a harder time than telephone workers, perhaps because they have been more personally identified with their work. Atchley writes, "People with few alternatives, those who have little money or poor health, who were over-involved in their jobs, who are unaccustomed to running their own lives, who experience other role losses in addition to retirement, who leave communities where they had lived for many years—these are the people who are apt to experience deep and lengthy periods of depression following the honeymoon period." Family members should be particularly watchful if their elders fall into one or more of these categories.

2. *Financial anxiety.* Though retired Americans tend to be better off financially than many other groups, most retirees will notice a reduction in actual income. The adjustment to a "fixed" income, in which earnings stay the same no matter what you do, may bring many initial uncertainties. When policymakers mention "fixed incomes," they seem to stress the negative—a mentality derived from the '60s and '70s, when inflation raged out of control. But fixed incomes have a plus side too: you will not get fired from Social Security! Nowadays, with Social Security and some pensions adjusted for the cost of living, the fear of inflation is considerably reduced.

Nonetheless, a large mental adjustment is necessary. The retired person goes from an economically active style to a passive one. Before, income depended on success at work. Now it stays the same, no matter what he does. The feeling may be one of helplessness, of lost control.

Financial anxiety can often be relieved by working through a budget. Retiring people are readily conscious that their income is going down. They may less readily assimilate other changes: fewer expenses (clothes and transportation for work, for example), and lower taxes. Social Security income is not taxed at all unless there are high earnings from other sources; earnings from pensions and investments are not subject to Social Security taxes. Many communities reduce property taxes too. Medical expenses will probably eventually rise, but Medicare will pay the lion's share of them. Finally, savings and long-term assets (such as a house) need not be saved into the grave; old age is what savings are for. A budget may serve to lessen anxiety.

What usually will not greatly relieve parents' anxiety is their children's assurance that "We will take care of you."

At this stage, most parents want to take care of themselves. They fear, as much as anything, "being a burden." They seek independence. Their children should honor that independence, and guard it.

In their early sixties, Bill and Emily moved into town from the farm they had worked for 38 years. They left their land to their only son, and found a place in a large city where they could be near a daughter who was going through a difficult divorce.

Bill and Emily are lifelong members of a strict, fundamentalist church. One of their daughters, Abbie, says she thinks Bill felt more responsibility for the church than he did for his own farm.

Growing up, his children were afraid of him. Bill was a silent, unemotional person who worked hard and could never bring himself to tell them he loved them. Emily was more outgoing, but without a sense of humor. She seemed to resent her life on the farm and the strictness of their church. When all three of the children rebelled and joined other churches, she actually seemed pleased.

It was pretty clear to the children that their parents' marriage was unhappy. Fortunately, though, each of them had a secure sense of being loved by their parents, though they missed their parents' love for each other. Occasionally, Bill would try to be affectionate toward Emily, but she would react stiffly. Emily once told Abbie, "You don't understand what I've been through. I'd have gotten a divorce if I didn't think it was wrong." But she never would discuss the matter beyond that.

In retirement, the two have grown further apart. Bill, now 77, has sunk into depression. Abbie calls him "a broken man." He no longer frightens his children, yet he can't break free of the past. Abbie often tells her father, "I love you, Dad." He says, "Thank you," which is as close as he can come to saying "I love you" in return.

At first Bill kept busy puttering around the house, but about a year ago he stopped. He became very quiet and sensitive to noise. He lost weight. After several of his closest friends died, Bill seemed to lose interest in life.

Emily isn't understanding. She sees Bill's depression as a sign of weakness, and if he speaks of his feelings she shoots him down. Amy, the daughter who lives nearest them, suggested that her father see a psychologist. Amy took Bill the first time, and he went quite willingly. Now he goes alone. Having someone to talk to has helped.

But Emily has her own problems. She was deeply affected when her sister died suddenly.

Abbie wonders if her parents' relationship will ever improve and realizes that it may not. They are each caught in a grief cycle, unable to help the other escape. She says, "I want them to be happy, but they've never thought happiness was a legitimate emotion. That's because they've never experienced freedom in Christ."

3. *Marital difficulties.* The greatest strain of retirement is often the changed relationship between husbands and wives. In one survey, 55 percent of the wives of retired men (and two-thirds of the wives of *early* retirees) regretted their husbands' retirement. This was particularly true in working-class homes. Ironically, while working-class husbands usually enjoy retirement more than other men, their presence at home all day seems to irritate their wives. It's as if they don't belong there.

Over the years, most married people have worked out a careful accommodation to each other. Each partner usually has his or her own turf—the husband's in the garden, the wife's in the kitchen, to use one common example. Suddenly, with retirement, the patterns change. I talked to one exasperated woman whose recently retired husband had taken over the checkbook, after years of letting her manage the family finances. Suddenly she didn't know what was going on anymore. Her husband volunteered no information about what he was doing about insurance and savings, areas in which she had developed definite opinions. But she didn't feel she could insist on being involved.

Added to this disruption, male-female roles often shift. Older men may allow impulses of tenderness and compassion to surface. They become less "father," with its aura of authority and objectivity, and more "grandfather," with its concerns for nurturing and encouragement. The posture of women may also change. Some feel freer to express "typically male" attitudes such as aggressiveness and authority. One small evidence of this is the number of older couples in which the wife takes over driving—a shift that might have been unthinkable in the earlier years of marriage. Women may also demand a say in some important decision, such as where to locate, or what kind of vacation to take. "For all these years I've done what you wanted to do," she may argue. "Now I want some say." Most couples make these readjustments smoothly, but there is always the possibility, especially in marriages where communication is weak, that they can be dramatically troublesome.

Overall, surveys suggest that good marriages will get better after retirement, but bad marriages, like Bill's and Emily's, may further deteriorate. Add illness of one of the partners, or any other source of stress, and the unhappiness increases.

Marital discord is the last complication children want to see in their aging parents' lives. Yet here, as elsewhere, the reality is that life after 65 is more challenging than the image of peaceful, nuturing grandparents would suggest.

Sometimes parents may want to talk about their marital problems, and adult children ought to try to listen sympathetically. They ought to be particularly careful, however, not to allow themselves to be used by one party against the other. It does not help for children to take sides. In fact, older couples may need professional counseling. If the marital problems require more time and expertise than a pastor can give, he may refer them to a psychologist or psychiatrist.

4. *Depression* is one of the plagues of old age. Psychiatrist Olga Knopf puts it bluntly: "Each aged individual is depressed at least part of the time."

I don't think this is an entirely bad thing. Since a person can cope with only so much stress and change, depression enables one to withdraw and meditate periodically. In this sense, depression may be a positive phenomenon—a natural body response to an overloaded system. A person who is mildly depressed for a brief period will often come out of depression with a fresh resolve to deal with problems creatively.

Chronic depression, however, has a very threatening side. Unable to relate to anything outside themselves, some people simply "give up."

A study by Dr. Marjorie Lowenthal indicates that depression is least problematic for those involved in close personal relationships. In Lowenthal's study, 45 percent of the women who had been widowed in the last seven years were depressed, but for those who had no confidant, 73 percent were depressed. The same pattern emerged among both men and women who were recently retired.

Lowenthal's research suggests a strategy for dealing with depression in older people: Work to increase their circles of interaction. Start with family. Make every effort to get the whole family involved in visiting "Grandpa." Young children, particularly, need not be whisked away from a depressed older person; they can perform an essential therapeutic role just by sitting in Grandpa's lap.

There is some evidence to suggest that ties with friends aid morale even more than contact with family members. While you cannot force two people to renew a friendship, you can sometimes make it easier. Provide stationery and stamps for letter-writing. Make the long-distance phone call on your own phone, while your mother is visiting. Invite the old friends to dinner along with your parents.

Work, finally, to involve the depressed person in some voluntary organization. This may be as simple as making sure he or she goes regularly to church, or to some midweek meeting. (A pastor can be helpful in strategizing what meetings are most likely to help.) Whether with the church or with the rest of the community, the key is usually an invitation. Your casual comment about the Men's Fellowship Breakfast is easily put off. But a peer's call and practical suggestion for follow-up is not so easy to turn down. "I thought you might enjoy the Men's Breakfast at the church next week. Why don't I stop by and pick you up?"

Children of a depressed parent will do better not to nag;

rather, they might try facilitating the right kinds of invitations by others. This is more difficult to manage from a distance, but a telephone call to a key individual—a pastor, or someone in an Area Agency on Aging—can supply some good leads as to whom to call next.

When a depressed person stops functioning normally—when there is weight loss, an extended withdrawal from relationships, a dramatic disruption of normal sleep patterns, or an inability to sustain normal activity—professional counseling is needed. Such extreme depression ought not to be ignored. It is not normal behavior and will not necessarily "work itself out." Outside intervention is needed, but the elderly person is often too depressed to make the effort to get help.

Wilfred Rankin was a high school principal in the days when principals had some authority. He ran a large school in a middle-sized town, and practically everybody knew him.

A kind man, with a strong sense of duty and self-discipline, Wilfred is past 80 now. Since retirement he has seemed happy enough with his quiet life of gardening, reading, and a smaller circle of friends. "Your values change tremendously as you grow older," he says. "Material things mean less. Somebody asked me, 'What do you want?' I don't want anything. That wouldn't have been true 30 years ago. At one time you had your heart set on being a member of this group or that group. Now you don't care."

He feels that he made a successful adjustment to retirement. "A lot of it," he explains, "is you set your mind ahead of time. If you didn't prepare for it, that would be difficult. Teachers often come up to me and say, 'I could retire next year. Do you have any advice?' I ask them, 'What hobbies do you have?' If they don't have any, I'll tell them, 'Then you'll wish you'd never retired!' I've always enjoyed my garden. The only times I get restless are on rainy days. So long as I can get outside, I'm fine."

Nonetheless, Wilfred looks back on some things he wishes he'd done differently. When he walked out the

door of the high school for the last time, his responsibilities went from 100 percent to zero. He thinks now
that it would have been easier to phase out gradually,
as some careers allow. "I have a friend who ran a lumber
yard. He still goes down there every day. I don't think
he does much, but he knows what's happening."

At the time of his retirement, a friend asked Wilfred
to come by and talk about a job. "I told him, 'I've
watched a clock for my whole life. I'm not going to do
that again.' Now I look back and wonder whether I
should have. If I had it to do over again, I'd get more
involved. I really thought at one time I'd do VISTA. I
kind of wish I had, so that I could have spent some years
doing something for somebody else, not myself. I think
a lot of people would do something like that if they got
a little push or encouragement from somebody who knew
more about it."

After Retirement, What Next?

After the initial transition, the first great task of retirement is to define what you are going to do with the rest of
your life. Most people have given little thought to this
problem since starting their career forty years before. Then,
making a living, caring for children, and keeping up a house
limited their options. In retirement there are generally
many more choices. A person can do practically anything—
from watching houseplants grow all day to hitchhiking to
Alaska! There's nobody to say you can't.

Hobbies, an active social life, sports, travel, gardening,
grandchildren—many retired people never slow down. Retirement offers the chance to do what they have been trying
to do in spare moments all through life. "I've always loved
to read," one woman in her seventies told me. "And now
I have time to read to my heart's content. It's wonderful!"

This is the typical pattern of the First Day: to be so busy

you feel your schedule is jammed. Many children of retired parents have found that they see far less of Mother and Dad than they expected, simply because Mother and Dad are too busy to fit them onto their calendar. Another woman said to me, "If I manage to do all the things I have planned, I'm going to have to live another forty years."

Yet free time lies heavily on some, and on their loved ones. Speaking of her recently retired parents, one young woman said, "I am their hobby and social function. I've let it get out of control. They've become too dependent on me and I on them." That is a nightmare, not only to children, but to most parents. "The last thing any parent wants," says Wilfred Rankin, "is to be a burden or to ask his kids for anything."

Hobbies are not necessarily a cure-all for such seniors. Hobbies are usually designed to give people a break from more strenuous pursuits. They are often, by design, frivolous. Some people aren't bothered by this in the least, but others feel purposeless, as though their hobbies were merely make work. The avid golfer may grow less avid when he plays every day.

Yet seniors often find it difficult to find and develop major new interests. Many lack the drive they once had; Wilfred's comment about "not wanting anything" reflects a common feeling. In his later years, Winston Churchill, who had a huge appetite for adventure as a young man, wrote, "It is hard to find new interests at the end of one's life."

So some older people, particularly those in poor health, do very little. One survey indicated that one-third of all free time is devoted to television. Ronald Blythe, in *The View in Winter*, quotes a British district nurse who remembered pre-TV days, when she would see the faces of the old staring out the window all day: "They're staring in now, aren't they—at the telly!" she says. "Half of them don't even know what the weather is outside."

The more active the retirement, the happier the retired person. So the literature of aging generalizes. But what kind of activities do busy retired people pursue? They fall into five general categories:

1. *Leisure-pleasure.* This includes travel, golf, card games, hobbies. Retirement communities seem to specialize in facilitating the pursuit of pleasure. What they really do is to facilitate society, something elders need increasingly as they grow older and their circle of friends begins to shrink.
2. *Family.* We expect grandparents to dote on their grandchildren, and they usually do. For some, grandchildren become virtually a career. (Great-grandparenting has also increased, since people live longer.) Grandparents can play an extremely helpful role in the lives of their grandchildren. In doing so, they express love for their own children as well; the grandchildren offer an "excuse" to grow closer.

   A warning is in order: the expectations can be oppressive. Conflicts about how children should be raised can be terribly emotional between, say, a mother and her own mother. And at least one study showed that older women who live near a married child with young children have lower morale than those who don't. The suspected culprit was too much babysitting. If small children are exhausting to parents in their twenties and thirties, then they are doubly so to grandparents in their sixties and seventies. Yet a grandparent may feel guilty about setting strict limits on how much babysitting he or she will provide.

   Still, grandchildren and other family ties are a great source of pleasure for many seniors. If distance separates them from their children, they will often invest substantial time traveling from one child's home to the next for extended stays. "Often they're checking out which kid to live near," says Elizabeth Wrightman. Whether this motive is a hidden part of the visit or not, family ties preoccupy many retired people.

3. *Friendships.* My father's dream of retired life is to travel around the country visiting all the people he and my mother have known through the years. That desire—to "catch up" on friendships—is a common part of retirement. While family ties predominate, some older people invest substantial time in friendships. They have lunch, or play golf, or take long walks.

Those who have lost spouses due to divorce or death particularly value friendships. They have time to invest, and they feel the need for intimacy. In my church there are four older women whom I admire immensely. They have done a great deal of traveling together, and stay in almost daily contact. They all seem to be enjoying old age, largely because of the pleasure they have received from these late-blooming friendships.

4. *Part-time work.* While most 65-year-olds are glad to retire, surveys also show that most would like to work on a part-time basis, to ease out gradually. Job-sharing is one fruitful possibility. I know two older women who split the work of a physician's office nurse for several years after they retired. Neither one wished to work full time, but sharing the job kept them in the working world, helped strengthen their own friendship, and provided needed income. Both of them are now fully retired, but fondly remember those transitional years.

Some firms have allowed top executives to retire from high-pressure positions and take lower-level jobs at a fraction of their former salary. In a way that often happens when such executives become "consultants" after retirement: they work under reduced responsibilities, have a more flexible schedule, and usually ease out of their work over a period of years.

Rarely, it seems, do older people fight to stay in power, unless they feel financially vulnerable. But many like to continue to feel useful on the job. Being paid for work is important to some, not merely because they need the money but because they need the status. For some, it would be more desirable to work at minimum wage in a department store, than to do far more interesting and demanding work for a community organization as a volunteer.

5. *Volunteering.* Many senior citizens occupy themselves as volunteers through their churches or in social service agencies or clubs. Community organizations that have traditionally relied on at-home mothers are turning to this growing group of people who really do have time and ability to give. The Louis Harris study estimated that many more seniors would like to volunteer than now do. But they lack knowledge of the opportunities, transportation, and sometimes reimbursement for meals or travel.

Born in West Virginia, Barbara Marks learned, the hard way, how to survive tough times. Her father was an alcoholic who, because he didn't like farming, sold the family holdings when his father and mother died. Then he lost all the money. Ashamed of himself, he left home to earn it back. He was found in a train station with a bullet hole in his temple. They called it a suicide, though the gun was never found.

Barbara began training as a nurse at the age of sixteen. The war years took her to California. There she married and had two sons, but divorced her husband when he couldn't quit his spendthrift habits. Though she retired from full-time nursing more than ten years ago, she has held various part-time jobs until recently. She is a no-nonsense, hardworking woman, fiercely independent. She maintains close ties with her two sons and their families, and she has a variety of enjoyable activities that occupy her time. But the critical factor in her happy retirement has been her church.

For most of her life she was a sporadic church attender of limited commitment. What she calls "my real church life" was formed in recent years, particularly through the influence of a woman named Kaye. "When I was tempted to shirk my responsibilities, she would very gently insist that I keep it up," Barbara recalls. As a nurse, often working nights, Barbara found it difficult to make it to church. But Kaye persisted.

Now she and Kaye are among the "fearsome foursome" of older women, whose friendship I mentioned earlier. They began traveling together. In their first major excursion, they joined a ship visiting denominational mission stations among the Indians of the Alaskan coast. It was hardly a luxury cruise. They slept in bunks and did their own cooking and clean-up. The travelers were of all ages, including nine teen-agers.

At the outset the kids admitted, "We don't know how to cook, but we do know how to clean up." So the fearsome foursome worked in teams to see that meals were made. At the end, when everyone was preparing to scatter in all directions for their homes in several states, the teenagers banded together and made a shy statement: "We just wanted you to know there wasn't any generation gap on this boat." Barbara has fond, proud memories of that experience.

Now the fearsome foursome have grown too old for much travel, but they continue as enthusiastic participants in church life. Barbara hosts a weekly Bible study that meets over breakfast in her mobile home. They have been at it for years, and Barbara finds her interest in the Bible continuing to deepen. It came late in life, and she is trying to make up for lost time. It is clearly, for her, sheer pleasure.

The Failure of Senior Hedonism

I have said that the first great task of retirement is to define what you will do with your life. It isn't enough, however, to merely pursue activities that make you happy or keep you busy. That, at any stage of life, would be frivolous. It would not satisfy the needs of the soul. We are called to take what God gives us in life and use it for others' good and for God's glory.

Sometimes seniors seem to be considered an exception to this rule. Having done their life's work, they can hang up their responsibilities. "Take it easy," their children urge. This well-meaning advice is usually just the opposite of what they need. It trivializes old age. It suggests that how seniors live makes no difference, as long as they are happy.

No doubt many elders practice Senior Hedonism with considerable success in their "young old" years. Nobody is jealous, really, of their trips and their hours of bridge and their pleasurable expenditures.

But Senior Hedonism fails on three counts. First, it often fails to forestall unhappiness. The superficiality eventually shows itself even to the hedonist. Second, it fails to reveal the dignity of old age. Dignity is, at all points in life, tied to higher aspirations than pleasing oneself. Finally, it fails to prepare for the challenges ahead. Seniors know that their hedonism cannot last. They see their friends falling into suffering and death. They pursue their pleasure while looking over their shoulders at the approach of the later days of the week.

What seniors need, on all three counts, is a vocation.

Finding a Vocation

Vocation is a word with a complicated history. It comes from the Latin *vocatus*, meaning "invitation" or "call." The apostle Paul gave *call* a specialized meaning. He wrote the Thessalonians about God's "call" to them "to be saved through the sanctifying work of the Spirit and through belief in the truth. He called you to this through our gospel, that you might share in the glory of our Lord Jesus Christ" (2 Thess. 2:13,14). God's call to every person, young or old, is to share in the glory of Jesus.

In the early and medieval church, this "vocation" became identified with monasticism. Someone answering God's call became a monk or a nun. Any other career choice fell short of God's glory.

But Martin Luther exploded that view, emphasizing that God's call to be a Christian must be answered in any and every situation in life—in carpentry, in farming, in business, in domesticity. Christians were called to reflect God's glory wherever they found themselves, in practical work as well as in worship. Unfortunately Luther's concept of "calling" eroded over time, and lost its Christian quality. A vocation became just a job.

Here is the problem: If elders are out of a job, are they also out of a vocation? In the modern, secularized sense of the word, yes. But the Christian sense of vocation is different. The question older people must ask is: Now that I have lived for 65 (or 75, or 85) years, have I completed my call? The answer must be: Never. In every circumstance we are called by God to share in his glory. We must grapple with the terribly difficult question: With what I have been given, what does God want me to do? And in what I do, how can I share in the glory of God?

Retired people may now be better able to answer that question than ever before. They are free, unhindered by schedules and responsibilities, or the need to please others. They can afford to take risks. Dr. Benjamin Spock, indicted at the age of 80 for his struggle against the war in Vietnam, put it well: "At my age, why should I be afraid to make public protests along with Stokely Carmichael?"

Paul Tournier tells the story of a man, depressed by his retirement, who went back to the bank where he had worked to do a little job classifying documents. His spirits lifted. "It did not require much to transfigure him," comments Tournier. "But for how long?" The problem had been postponed, but not solved.

Seniors should search for vocations that do more than postpone their problems, keeping them busy and propping up their ego. Rather than holding on to a piece of their old security, seniors should look for a new purpose, one that will last. "We need people," writes T. Herbert O'Driscoll in the book, *Affirmative Aging,* "who are the memories of neighborhoods and families and labor unions and churches. We need those who remember segregation and the Holocaust, Hiroshima, and a nation without Social Security and the Salk vaccine."

Vocations Can Be Close to Home

It is easiest to think of a retirement vocation in terms of new careers. Elders may consider joining the Peace Corps, or becoming short-term missionaries in Borneo or Ghana. They may launch new organizations. (Maggie Kuhn started Gray Panthers after she retired.) They may become involved in projects they have always longed to try. One retired engineer I know has invested his considerable abilities in inventing a better wheelchair. A physicist is, after a lifetime of teaching, enjoying a semi-communal lifestyle where he experiments with solar heating and faithfully participates in peace marches.

Other choices would keep you nearer to home, in less remarkable but no less meaningful activities: serving in your church, joining a Foster Grandparent program, serving meals in a soup kitchen. Every community in America offers a wide array of such possibilities, where an elder can give his time and energy, and enjoy the company of others.

Barbara Marks is not so unusual in finding her new vocation within her church. Most older Americans do attend church and consider their faith significant, though this seems obscure in the literature on aging. (For instance, studies show that 5–15 percent of older people participate in senior centers or groups, while 61 percent attend church regularly; but there are whole chapters written on the significance of senior centers for every page written about the significance of church.) For elders the church should become, not merely a place to attend, but a place to exercise their vocation.

Ed Powers, a gerontologist at Iowa State, emphasizes the potential of church programs geared for seniors. "Now you can say, 'We're going to get together two nights a week,' and nobody says, 'We need babysitters.' We don't have people saying, 'I can't do that because I work until seven o'clock.' The opportunity exists for servanthood and spiritual development on a scale that we have not envisioned."

Yet it is often the old who disqualify themselves. "There are two barriers I've seen from the start," says David Jobe, pastor for senior adult ministries at First Evangelical Free Church in Fullerton, California. "One is, 'I *won't* get involved because I've done my part.' The other is, 'I *can't*. I couldn't do that, I'm too old for that.'"

"Often older people pull back in retirement and rest," notes Janine Tartaglia, of Pasadena's First Nazarene Church. "That's okay. There's a place for rest. We need to retreat. But we need to remember that we shouldn't go into retreat forever." As it was for Barbara Marks, so it will be for many elderly people: the persistent encouragement of another person will provide the key to their involvement. Their children can often be those encouragers. If they cannot, someone else can. Barbara's case is not unusual in this way also: another elder can move an elderly person into action.

A word of warning: Children cannot assume that their parents' God-given calling is to babysit. It may be that their parents will leave the area altogether to serve in some mission or volunteer program in another country or another state. It may be that their parents will open themselves to stress and danger that seems inconceivable. Children who care about their parents' vocation will have to give them the freedom to find it.

Making a Vocation When You Don't Have a Choice

It is exciting to think of going to Borneo, or designing a new wheelchair. Yet many seniors will foresee no possibility of such new activities; they will find their time and energy taken up by responsibilities they have not chosen. They may long for a "vocation," but find themselves tied to mundane chores—caring for a sick spouse, for instance, or nursing their own health. Luther's emphasis should help here. He said that we most often find our vocation within the circumstances we are given. Farmers should not look to the monastery; they should look to farming. So many elders will find their vocation within a life they can hardly avoid.

Most seniors will see grandchildren, for instance, as a given responsibility. You do not choose to be a grandparent—the choice is made for you. Since this is such a significant "given" for most seniors, let us look at it more closely as a possible vocation.

Many grandparents enjoy their grandchildren, but not all treat grandparenting as a vocation. Some simply indulge themselves. They enjoy their role; they like buying pretty dresses and elaborate toys and taking their grandchildren on outings. They do it because they like to (or don't do it because they don't like to), regardless of the effect on the child.

Other grandparents, however, have learned to treat their role as a vocation. They understand what a grandparent can do for a child. Grandparents have time that harried parents do not. They live outside the power conflicts that parents and children contend with. Thus, grandparents can provide nurture in an intimate and relaxed style.

Through storytelling, grandparents can link grandchildren to their roots. They can help the grandchildren gain understanding of their own parents (who, grandparents remind them, were also once children). My own children are particularly interested in stories my mother or father tell about my childhood—especially times when I was naughty and got punished.

Divorce opens up a powerful vocation for grandparents. The odds are today that most parents will see the failure of the marriage of at least one of their children. Grandparents can be particularly important to their grandchildren at such times. A divorce often leaves parents with little extra energy to give, causing their children additional deep insecurity. Grandparents can provide a sense of stability and hope—a refuge for their grandchildren in troubled circumstances.

Many children are deeply affected by a grandparent's intimacy with God; indeed, the conventional childhood image of God as a grandfather cannot be completely accidental. Because grandparents do not have to involve themselves in power struggles about whether to make a child attend Sunday night youth fellowship, they can model a very positive faith. (On the other hand, grandparents who model a narrow-minded, mechanical religiosity can have an equally negative spiritual impact.) My grandfather, even when he was very sick, left an indelible impression on my spirit; he affected me more than any individual beside my parents. In that respect I am hardly alone. It is astonishing how often people mention their grandparents when describing how they came to faith in God.

It should be noted that grandchildren will, in our time, rarely be babies by the time their grandparents retire. The average woman is 46 when her first grandchild is born. Eighty percent of all women have a grandchild by their mid-fifties. This means grandparents over 65 will usually deal with adult or adolescent grandchildren.

It's possible, though, that grandparents may help adolescents even more than they help small children. Older grandchildren are more likely to gain from the wisdom of their grandparents, especially if they have trouble communicating with their parents—which they often do.

In grandparenting we can see that vocation depends less on a person's role than on how he or she perceives the role. Becoming a grandparent takes no talent, except for reproduction; but to understand yourself as a servant to your grandchildren you have to share at least a little in Jesus' character. To that extent, you share in his glory. We know how Jesus opened his arms to children, welcoming them. Grandparents can do the same, and with the same motive.

Spiritual Values

A vocation may come through new choices, or it may be discovered within given responsibilities. Either way, seniors will need to shift into a new set of values.

If their emphasis remains on what they can do, then older people are bound to be constant losers. At 65 they may be able to do a great deal; at 75 they will almost certainly be able to do less, and at 85 they may be unable to do much at all. Will they lose their vocation? If they can no longer go to Borneo, must they settle for second best? If the emphasis is on such spiritual values as love, intimacy, courage and godliness, then elders need not lose at all. They may gain.

Spiritual values keep their significance even after strength flags and health is gone. Simone de Beauvoir, surveying anthropological studies, observes that not all cultures hold their elderly dear: "If a community is merely trying to subsist from day to day, a member who becomes a useless mouth that has to be fed is in decline. But if this community . . . desires to live on spiritually, then it looks upon the ancient man, who belongs both to the past and to the after-world, as its embodiment. In this case even the utmost possible degree of physical decay may be looked upon as the highest point of life."

Elders have value to those whom they love, even when they are physically unable to accomplish anything practical. They can be a living sign for anyone who cares to read: Life is more than a job, for it continues long after jobs are impossible. To be that living sign, witnessing to values that come from another world—that is surely the ultimate vocation.

The First Day
Continued:
Practical Matters

THE AGE OF 65 IS THE GATEWAY TO THE WORLD of leisure and freedom, and so introduces broad new questions of life direction and vocation. Sixty-five is also the gateway to Social Security and life on a "fixed income." It introduces new practical issues, such as how to make sense of Medicare regulations, or whether you wish to make a living will. In this chapter I will attempt to summarize the way the Social Security system works. I will also suggest a number of legal or quasi-legal preparations that ought to be made during the First Day.

A full discussion of retirement finances is beyond the scope of this book, as is a full discussion of the remarkably complicated Social Security rules and regulations. An overall grasp of the issues can be helpful, however. Since regulations and benefits change frequently, any specific dollar amounts mentioned will soon be out of date. I give them in 1989 figures in order to provide some idea of their relative value.

Retirement Finances

It has been stated that the current generation of Americans over 65 are, overall, the most financially secure in history. Government spending has made all the difference. About a third of the federal budget goes to the elderly; government spending in this area—federal, state and local—is about three times what is spent by government on youth and children, including the costs of education.

Generally, the financial condition of older persons can be described as follows: Well off are the white "young old" (under 75) who are married, in good health, and have pensions or investments. Truly poor are the non-white "old old" (over 85) who are in poor health, widowed, isolated, and are living on Social Security alone. Over 90 percent of the elderly poor are unmarried women. (About two-thirds of all women are widows by the time they reach 75.)

As a rule of thumb, one may say: Social Security, as a sole source of income, will enable an older person to survive, but he or she (usually she) will be quite poor. Add a pension or some other source of income to Social Security, and life looks considerably brighter. Children trying to evaluate their parents' finances without being too nosy can start with these rough criteria.

What about savings? Most older Americans have managed to save a little, but these savings are usually a minor part of their financial picture. Their greatest tangible asset is normally their home. A remarkable two-thirds of all elderly Americans own their own homes. The free-and-clear home, however, may not be so great a financial boon as it appears. Many of these houses are old and poorly maintained and are expensive to repair and heat.

Seniors who own or nearly own a home have two options for improving their income. They can sell their home and (without paying taxes on the capital gains) move into rental housing or another, smaller home with lower maintenance costs. The remaining cash can be invested for extra income. Another possibility is the reverse annuity mortgage—essentially a home mortgage in reverse. In a normal home mortgage, the bank pays out one lump sum to buy a house, and then must be repaid month by month. In a reverse annuity mortgage the bank pays out month by month—sometimes a set sum, sometimes as a flexible line of credit—and must be repaid in one lump sum at death or the termination of the loan (when the house is sold).

Older people often feel financially insecure, whether they are or not. Some feel a powerful temptation to put their savings into "too good to be true" investment opportunities. Such investments seem to offer seniors an escape from their poverty, as well as a sense of controlling their own destiny. Unfortunately, such investment opportunities usually *are* too good to be true. The fact that the person offering the opportunity is a Christian, or is sincere, proves very little about the quality of the investment. Financial planners usually suggest that older people put their investments in secure, highly liquid investments such as certificates of deposit.

Elders who have little savings and no pension usually either continue working as much as possible, rely on relatives, or make do on food stamps. In fact, "make do" is what most do. Relatives, though they often provide care for the elderly, rarely provide significant amounts of income. With the current financial picture, they have not needed to. The best guess is that Social Security will not run into difficulty until about 2020; after that, the financial needs of the elderly may become, as in the past, a significant family obligation.

Social Security and Medicare

Two factors increase the difficulties of elders dealing with finances. First, the elderly often have less energy to confront problems. Second, their problems tend to cluster in the large bureaucracies of the Social Security Administration.

There is no special secret to penetrating this maze, apart from persistence. Since elderly people often lack the energy and nerve to tackle the bureaucracy, the task sometimes falls to their children. It is helpful to have some overall grasp of how Social Security and Medicare work. I will attempt to explain that now.

Social Security and Medicare are administered together. If you think of the Social Security Administration as the elder's employer, you can think of Social Security payments as his salary, and Medicare as his company's health insurance plan. People receive different "salaries" from Social Security depending on how much they or their spouses contributed during their working lives; but all "employees" get the same health coverage from Medicare.

When elders choose to begin receiving Social Security, they are automatically enrolled in Medicare. (Those who aren't eligible for Social Security—usually those who worked for the government, or have never worked at all— can still enroll separately for Medicare, though the cost is substantial.)

The most important choice an elder makes regarding Social Security is when to begin receiving payments. The timing makes a substantial difference in how large those payments will be. The current law rewards you for each year you delay, and that reward is growing. At this writing, a person waiting to retire at 70 rather than 65 sees his checks increase by 15 percent (3 percent a year); by 2008, the increase is expected to reach 40 percent. The only way to be precise about the choice is to ask the Social Security Administration to calculate benefits for retirement at several different ages. Financial planners say that someone working part-time or less from age 62 on is probably wise to receive payments immediately and invest the money. (They assume he has the will power to save it rather than spend it.) For those still working full-time, it's definitely best to wait, because there is a penalty of $1 for every $2 earned over a certain low figure ($8,800 in 1988, and rising with the cost of living). After age 70 ½, there is no advantage from waiting, for seniors can earn all they want from other sources without penalty.

To begin receiving Social Security payments, you must apply *in writing* at a local Social Security office. You will be expected to produce your Social Security number, proof of your age (a birth certificate, passport, etc.), a marriage certificate, W-2 forms for the past two years, and proof of military service, if applicable. Someone applying for benefits after the death of a spouse needs the same material.

Social Security payments are not large—the average in 1989 is $537 a month for a single person; over $921 for a couple. But since this money is not taxable for those who earn less than $25,000 a year in other income ($32,000 for couples), and since Social Security payments are no longer deducted, for most people these payments are comparable to ordinary income between 25 and 40 percent higher. Thus the average couple's benefit is equivalent to at least $1,100 per month in preretirement income.

By current law, widowed spouses who didn't work outside

the home receive about 70 to 75 percent of the Social Security benefits earned by their deceased spouses.

The government has a "safety net" for poor elderly people who are ineligible for Social Security or whose total income, including SS benefits, falls below a very low amount. The scheme is known as SSI (Supplemental Security Income). As of 1989 the maximum benefit was $368 per month, or $553 for couples. You apply for SSI at the same Social Security office, using a separate form. You need to show evidence of current income, papers itemizing your assets, your latest rent receipt or your latest tax bill on your home, and information about your spouse's income and assets.

A person who qualifies to receive Social Security benefits is usually earning too much to be eligible for SSI, unless his benefits are very low. In that case, SSI will only add a very small supplement, but makes him eligible to receive Medicaid and food stamps—very valuable benefits.

Medicare's Web of Regulations

Medicare is considerably more complicated than Social Security. Its regulations are constantly shifting, so it is virtually impossible to be sure exactly what an elder should rightfully receive. Rules are interpreted by fallible administrators, who don't always get it right. Children of elderly people can often help them untangle the bureaucratic web.

The best way through the web, however, is to have expert guidance. Since doctors in the U.S. receive a large share of their income through Medicare, most doctors' offices become quite adept at unraveling the web. If a senior's doctor "accepts assignment"—I will explain this phrase later on—he or she will do all or nearly all the paperwork for you, and will take up your cause with the administration. Even a doctor who does not accept assignment should have someone in his office who can help to interpret Medicare regulations. If you have Medigap insurance, the insurance company, in conjunction with the doctor's office, should work out your problems with the government.

Medicare comes in two parts, conveniently labeled "A" and "B." "A" covers all hospital bills, after a deductible of $564 (in 1988) for as long as an elder needs to be hospitalized.

"A" also pays for 150 days a year in a skilled nursing home. This is strictly for recovery from illness, not long-term care. The patient pays 20 percent of the first eight days, and the government pays the rest. "A" also pays for unlimited home health care if prescribed by a doctor. The emphasis is on *health* care, usually provided by an agency that specializes in home health care.

Under this plan Medicare will pay for visits by therapists and nurses, as well as for medical supplies and equipment. It will pay for hospice costs of dying patients. As of 1990 it will pay for 80 hours per year of housekeeping, meals, or other services that enable many elderly people to stay in their homes rather than go to nursing home facilities. The 80 hours is meant to give caregivers an occasional break. For similar reasons, Medicare will pay for 38 days a year of skilled home nursing care, beginning in 1990. Even though home care is often cheaper than a nursing home, the government is unlikely to cover a great deal more of these expenses in the foreseeable future. What they fear is that, once they open the door to such care, everybody over 65 will pour through it. What person, of any age, wouldn't like to have someone come in to cook meals and clean house? People rarely abuse nursing home services, but home care might be an infinitely costly burden for the government to assume.

If you think of "A" as hospitals, think of "B" as doctors.

Whether the doctor is helping in the hospital or in his office, his bill falls under "B" and is only partially covered. The senior pays a monthly premium (in 1989, usually deducted from the Social Security check) to Medicare plus an income tax surcharge if he or she makes over $10,000. In return, Medicare will pay 80 percent of "reasonable" doctor charges, and 100 percent after the patient has paid out $1,370 in a year.

The term "reasonable" is why half the nation's doctors refuse to "take assignment." "Taking assignment" means that a doctor agrees to bill Medicare directly and charge his patient only 20 percent of whatever amount Medicare deems reasonable. In other words, he agrees to be paid according to Medicare's scale. It's obvious why so many doctors object. Nor do they want to hire an extra employee just to do the paperwork for Medicare patients. In my middle-class community, with sixty internists listed in the yellow pages, I am told that only one such doctor will take assignment.

If a doctor doesn't take assignment, the patient must generally pay his entire bill and then fill out a form for reimbursement. Medicare will pay 80 percent of whatever part of the bill they think is reasonable, which is usually less than 80 percent of the bill.

There are long lists of what "B" will pay for and what it won't. Routine exams, eyeglasses, hearing aids, and drugs are probably the most significant items *not* covered. Beginning in 1991, drugs will be partly covered. A person will pay the first $600, then half the remaining cost.

Between deductibles, monthly payments, uncovered items, and the 20 percent copayment for all doctor bills, health care costs can be very substantial for senior citizens. An extended nursing home stay can eat up Medicare coverage entirely and wipe out finances. In this case, the Social

Security Administration has a safety net plan so that no elderly person need be without medical care or a place in a nursing home. It is called "Medicaid."

Safety Nets and Medigap Insurance

As SSI is to Social Security, so Medicaid is to Medicare. In fact, you apply for Medicaid in the same way you apply for SSI. Medicaid is administered by the states, and the benefits differ substantially from state to state—an issue worth investigating, for low-income elders who may be considering a move. Basically, Medicaid is designed to cover medical costs that Medicare won't. The catch is, you have to be, or become, very poor to qualify. Present regulations allow you to keep a car, your home, and a small savings account. You must spend all other financial resources first, before the government takes over. When you die, the government will usually collect your remaining assets, so you leave nothing to your heirs.

A typical case is a person of modest resources who enters a nursing home after being in the hospital. Medicare pays for 150 days, and this person's savings may be enough to pay for another four months. After nine months, his money runs out and he applies for SSI and Medicaid. For the rest of his life, his bills will be paid by the government. A very large percentage of those in nursing homes have become covered by Medicaid, meaning that most of their assets, apart from a house and a car, are gone. In many cases, these must be sold after their death, and the proceeds dedicated to the nursing home costs.

There is an alternative to this procedure—"Medigap" insurance. This is a health insurance policy designed to pay for those health costs that Medicare will not. The policies differ considerably; some cover only extra hospital and doctor costs, and some cover nursing homes as well (for higher premiums). Medigap policies cost roughly $500 to $1,000 a year, depending on the coverage.

Experts agree that the best Medigap plans are those that are available from the same company that covered you on the job, before retirement. You can usually continue to be covered *as long as you apply for continued coverage before your retirement.* If you miss that opportunity, you are on your own. When buying a Medigap policy, it would be a good idea to enlist the support of a friend who knows insurance well, for comparisons are quite tricky.

Making a Will

In theory, plans for death and disability ought to have been made years before retirement. After all, you do not have to be 65 to die. In practice, retirement pushes a person's thoughts forward, to the time of death. What has always been theoretically possible begins to seem like something you can bank on. Older Americans gradually become psychologically prepared to think through their own deaths.

They do so, however, on their own schedule. If they are not ready to make their plans and thus to deal practically with their deaths, family members cannot make them ready by nagging. Tactful suggestions can be made and proper resources made available. Finally, though, these matters are as personal as are matters of faith. Each person must prepare for death in his or her own way.

Wills, along with all other preparations for death, are valuable not merely in their practical significance—they do make things much easier for the survivors—but in their spiritual significance. In the Middle Ages, when modern wills were invented, they were not primarily legal documents at all. A will was a religious document, meant to demonstrate that a thoughtful Christian had faced his death in a Christian manner. Through it a church member would publicly confess his faith, acknowledge his sins, and deal with his property in such a manner that he showed a certain detachment from material things. (Often medieval Christians made very large gifts to the church, which was one way in which the church grew so wealthy.) It was considered extremely sinful to die without a will, for a will was the outward demonstration of an important inner reality—dealing with death.

Nowadays wills seem to have little to do with faith in God, and a lot to do with faith in good lawyers. Nonetheless, they can and do serve a religious function. They remain a means by which people come to terms with the fact that they will die. That is why older people—and younger people—find it so difficult to "get around" to making wills. The families of elderly people should try to be sensitive to this dimension.

While some older persons will procrastinate precisely because they are not yet ready to look death in the face, others will respond in just the opposite way, taking great pleasure in carefully planning their estate. This, too, can be exasperating to family members, if they think the old man or woman has grown obsessed with money. Money, however, is rarely the issue; power is at stake, for a person who is rapidly losing power. The will enables an elder to continue to outlive himself, in a sense—to influence future generations—by blessing children and grandchildren and philanthropic causes, and by demonstrating stern disapproval of certain errant relations. Even if very few elders actually make dramatic gestures through their wills, they feel that potentiality when other potencies are fading fast.

So much has been written about the importance of wills that surely no more need be said. Unfortunately, however, many if not most people still die before making a will, and according to an article in the *Wall Street Journal*, lawyers are among the worst at putting it off. Wills are particularly important for large estates, or for those who want to leave money to some charitable cause. Even for those of modest means, a will speeds the legal process and usually makes it less difficult and expensive. And a well-drafted will may prevent bickering and hurt feelings among those left behind.

As part of the legal will, or as a separate non-binding document, an older person may wish to decide what relatives should inherit personal belongings. If Sister is to get the rolltop desk, it helps to say so in writing, so that there is no possibility of misinterpretation. My own grandmother had verbally promised a beloved pearl ring to three different grandchildren. "We buried it with her," my mother says, "which was the smartest thing we ever did."

Selecting a Doctor

Since health problems are often the greatest difficulty of old age, the right doctor is imperative. An older person should never wait until he is very sick to find that doctor. Ideally, the doctor and patient should have established a comfortable way of communicating long before a crisis. The doctor should have gained, through a checkup, good basic information about the patient's normal blood pressure, weight, allergies, and medical history, and know what kind of treatment his patient wishes in life-threatening situations.

I have already mentioned the question of whether a doctor will "accept assignment." This important financial consideration ought to be weighed before a crisis arises.

Another important issue is what kind of doctor is desirable. Some doctors, particularly internists, practice medicine on elderly people a great deal more than others, and develop a certain amount of expertise. In addition, some doctors and clinics specialize in geriatric medicine. During the last three decades a great deal has been learned about the special health problems of older people, but not all doctors are equally knowledgeable or competent.

There is value in having a doctor who is familiar with geriatric medicine, but perhaps even more value in having a qualified doctor with whom you communicate well. Doctoring older people often takes time, and not all doctors will give it. A rule of thumb is that a physician ought to give an older person about an hour on the first visit. Anything much less, and he or she is not likely to have a complete picture of a senior's needs. But regardless of the time allotted, ask yourself: Did I feel rushed? Did I feel free to ask questions? Did I understand the answers? If you don't feel entirely comfortable, try someone else. It's worth the trouble and expense, for it can save a great deal more trouble and expense at a later, more critical time.

Durable Power of Attorney

The durable power of attorney (DPA) is a flexible legal instrument, authorizing someone you trust to make decisions regarding health care, finances, and other matters in the event that you are unable to make those decisions yourself. It is usually written to take effect only under certain specific conditions, and the limits on the powers can be carefully spelled out.

If an older person suffers, let us say, an incapacitating stroke, and has no DPA, his affairs may remain in limbo until a court declares him incompetent and names a guardian. A DPA allows him to choose, in advance, a spouse, child, sibling or other person, and defines just what kinds of decisions that person would be empowered to make. The DPA generally ends when the disabled person recovers, or when he dies. You need to see an attorney to make a DPA, for there are many variations on its powers, and it needs to be skillfully drafted.

Living Wills

A living will is a legal or quasi-legal document, indicating the kind of medical care you would like to have if you reach a point where you can no longer state your preference regarding being kept alive via "artificial" means. Typically, a living will instructs the doctor and all other health care professionals not to use respirators or other medical technology to preserve your life if the chances of your full recovery are remote and death is imminent in any case. Most states have given living wills legal status. Often specific wording is required. (For forms appropriate in each state, you can write The Society for the Right to Die, Room 323, 250 W. 57th St., New York, NY 10107.)

As one example, here is the Living Will form used in the state of Washington:

I, being of sound mind, willfully and voluntarily make known my desire that my life shall not be artificially prolonged under the circumstances set forth below, and do hereby declare that:

(a) If at any time I should have an incurable injury, disease or illness certified to be a terminal condition by two physicians, and where the application of life-sustaining procedures would serve only to artificially prolong the moment of my death, and where my physician determines that my death is imminent, whether or not life-sustaining procedures are utilized, I direct that such procedures be withheld or withdrawn, and that I be permitted to die naturally.

(b) In the absence of my ability to give directions regarding the use of such life-sustaining procedures, it is my intention that this directive shall be honored by my family and physician(s) as the final expression of my legal right to refuse medical or surgical treatment and I accept the consequences from such refusal.

(c) If I have been diagnosed as pregnant and that diagnosis is known to my physician, this directive shall have no force or effect during the course of my pregnancy.

(d) I understand the full import of this directive and I am emotionally and mentally competent to make this directive.

A durable power of attorney can be used either as an alternative, or as an addition to a living will. (State law varies. In some states, a living will is the only means by which a person can choose not to have maximum medical intervention. No one can be given such powers through a DPA.)

Some people object to living wills, because it is so difficult to consider in advance all medical possibilities (a living will offers little or no flexibility according to circumstances), or because they fear that the living will might tend to encourage lackluster medical performance, or because they consider it ethically dubious to fail to protect life with all our powers regardless of circumstances.

Whether or not you choose a living will, the most important action you can take is to discuss these issues with your physician. Let him or her know your preferences, and take time to discuss the situation as you imagine it. A written document—a living will, or a non-binding statement of preference, or a DPA—should be given to your doctor to keep in your file.

Funeral Arrangements in Advance

For the sake of their survivors, some people write out their preferences for a funeral service long before it is needed. This form can be followed:

Dear Loved Ones:
This letter is not a legal document, but merely a guide to my wishes:
I do/do not have a prearranged funeral service with a funeral home. It is with_____funeral home.
My preference is to be: Cremated_____; Ashes scattered_____; Buried_____; Embalmed_____

I prefer:
Closed casket_____; Open casket_____
Funeral service_____; Family graveside_____;
Memorial service_____
In my church_____; Funeral home_____;
Elsewhere_____; No service_____
I want a financially minimal funeral arrangement___;
I leave the financial arrangements to my survivors' discretion._____
These Scriptures and/or writings have meant much to me:_____

These hymns and/or songs have meant much to me:_____

I would like, if possible, those at my service to sing:___
_____

I would prefer remembrances to be (e.g., flowers, charitable gifts):_____

Other preferences and requests:_____
_____

Access to Information and Money

Most people, particularly if they have charge of the family financial affairs, keep a good deal of important information in their heads. When they die or become very sick, that information is suddenly inaccessible.

If a senior has a safe deposit box where important documents are stored, someone else should know where that box is located, and have legal access to it. In addition, it is extremely helpful if a person the senior trusts—a spouse, child, estate executor, or all three—has a joint bank account with the senior. Otherwise, family members will have to pay immediate expenses out of their own pockets, as there will be no money available.

It helps to write out key information, and give copies to several people—spouse, children, executor of your estate, clergyman. The following should be covered:

Executor of Will _____
Address _____
Phone _____

Physician _____
Address _____
Phone _____

Clergyman _____
Address _____
Phone _____

Lawyer _____

Address _____

Phone _____

Accountant _____

Address _____

Phone _____

Insurance Agent _____

Address _____

Phone _____

Investment Advisor _____

Address _____

Phone _____

Banks with Account Numbers _____

_____

IRAs, Keoughs, Pensions _____

_____

Where can the following be found?

Safe deposit box # _____

Location _____

Who has access? _____

Who has key? _____

Current Will _____

Insurance Policies (life, health, accident, home, other) _____

_____

_____

Stocks and Bonds _____

_____

Trust Agreements _____

_____

Bank Passbooks _____

_____

Tax Returns _____

_____

Contracts and Business Agreements _____

_____

Real Estate and Condominiums, Deeds, Title Policies
and Leases: _____

_____

_____

Jewelry and Other Valuables _____

_____

Financial Records (cancelled checks, etc.) _____

_____

Cemetery Plot Location: _____

Funeral Home: _____

Birth, Marriage, Divorce, Military Discharge, Adoption, Naturalization Certificates: _____

_____

_____

Passports _____

Vehicle Titles and Registrations _____

_____

Powers of Attorney _____

Name of Attorney in Fact _____

Keys (to buildings, vehicles, boats, safes, etc.) ____

_____

Day 2

MEMO TO MY MOTHER-IN-LAW

WE WERE LIVING IN NAIROBI WHEN WE GOT news of your first episode, Ozzie. We didn't know what to make of it; we were so far away, so removed from the situation.

You had been shopping at Sears when you became confused and disoriented. Somehow you managed to call home and tell Inell that you needed help. Henry rushed to the mall and found you, weak and befuddled. There wasn't, the doctors said later, a thing they could find wrong with you, except for those minutes you were unable to locate your car, unable to fix yourself firmly in time.

Then—was it weeks later?—it happened again. You were driving a handful of friends home from a luncheon when you lost all sense of where you were. You made it home before you collapsed. Inell innocently showed you a letter we had written, and you snapped impatiently, "I don't know them."

Again, the tests. Again, the diagnosis which is no diagnosis: "There's nothing wrong with you."

Seven years have gone by without another occurrence. You're as vital as a hummingbird. The only lasting reminder is the aspirin you take every day to keep your blood from clotting.

Yet those brief episodes moved the whole family into a different

79

view of our future. We had never seriously considered that you, of all people, would grow old. Now, since those episodes, we know. Though they left no discernible evidence in your health, they made a lasting difference in us. We heard the first rumble of distant thunder.

The Second Day: Beginnings of Reflection

ARLENE HAD ALWAYS SAID THAT SHE WOULD dread a mastectomy. Then, in her late sixties, she discovered a lump. Her doctor said surgery was indicated.

There was a tumor in only one breast, but the doctor was concerned about the risk of further cancer. "Let's just go in and take them both," he said to her. "You're over 65. What does it matter?"

It mattered a great deal to Arlene. She was incensed. Her daughter-in-law had been operated on not long before, and the doctors had done what they called a "lumpectomy." Wouldn't that be possible, since the tumor was small? But, because of the location of the tumor, the doctor said he would have to do a complete mastectomy.

Arlene insisted, and got her doctor's partner to listen to her. The partner promised he would try to do what she asked, though the final determination could only be made in the operating room.

Before the operation Arlene's daughter Suzy called from the west coast. Arlene, a longtime widow, sounded nervous and alone. Suzy thought about flying out to help, but decided she could be of more use later, during the recovery phase.

The morning after surgery, Arlene sounded chipper over the phone. She told Suzy, "They did it like I asked them to. They just took the lump."

The following morning, after the bandages were removed, Arlene's voice sounded listless. The doctors had taken far more of her breast than she had expected. Suzy listened to Arlene's description and then said, "Really, I'm just glad you're alive." She mentioned a young friend who had recently died of breast cancer.

"Yes," Arlene agreed. "I know I'm lucky to be alive."

"You've got a lot of people—two daughters and grandchildren—who love you and need you!" Suzy said. "Why, there are four people in this house who are crazy about you!"

"I know." Arlene's voice broke. "That's what I'm hanging on to."

When she hung up, Suzy was particularly troubled that her mother was so isolated. A relative had told Arlene frightening stories about the follow-up radiation treatments. No one seemed available to give her either encouragement or reliable information, and she was too far from home for visitors.

Suzy wondered whether she had made a mistake in not going to be with her mother. After thinking for a few minutes, she called the American Cancer Society in the city where Arlene was hospitalized. She told the woman who took her call about her mother's depression.

Then she called Ralph, the man her mother had been

dating, and asked, "Would you mind if I were very open and blunt?" Suzy was certain that he would lose interest in her mother after the breast surgery.

"I'd prefer it," he said.

"Do you love my mom?" Suzy asked. Ralph said he did. "Then she needs to know it. She's very depressed. They took more of her breast than she thought they would."

"Well, she's no less of a woman because of that." Ralph hesitated. "I'm not too good around hospitals, but I told her I'd take care of her house and yard."

"Good, that's one way of showing love," Suzy said. "I just wanted to let you know what has happened so you can be prepared. I don't know how she'll handle this."

That evening, when Suzy called her mother, she sounded much less depressed. An American Cancer Society representative had called and made an appointment to see her. Ralph, too, had called, had said he missed her, and that he was taking care of the yard. Twice he had told her he loved her.

An Invisible Beginning

The Second Day—the Day of Reflection—often dawns subtly. All the other days of old age are marked by some clear, external sign—retirement, or a spouse's death, or the need for daily help. But Day Two is internal, and often quite invisible. Even the aging person may be imperfectly aware of the changes happening inside.

For most, the First Day—Freedom Day—has been a surprisingly happy phase. Active retired people work hard at "staying young." Their families marvel: "Grandma just wears us all out!" This stage can seem as though it will last forever. Yet it always does end—soon for some, late for others. The Second Day often begins with a sudden crisis, when it first becomes clear that loss is unavoidably part of old age.

For Arlene, the loss was not merely tissue; it was her sense of womanhood. It suggested an end to her vitality as an attractive, desirable person. Her doctor's insensitivity drove the point home: She was finished as a woman. What loomed most terrifyingly was not cancer, but an image of herself as a dried-up old woman.

The elder may recover completely from a first shock. Everything may seem to return to normal. Yet the elder begins to think: The world is tilting on its axis away from summer, toward winter.

Novelist Jean Rhys described it this way: "Age seldom arrives smoothly or quickly. It's more often a series of jerks. After the first you slowly recover. You 'learn to live with the consequences.' Then comes another and another. At last you realize that you'll never feel perfectly well again, never be able to move easily; or see or hear well."

Until the first shock, most retired parents will not wrap their lives around their children. They may even, as we have seen, fiercely maintain their independence. Their friends may be more important to their well-being than are their children.

When older people are shaken by loss, however, family members gain importance—especially family members who make themselves available at the time of need. No one can schedule a crisis; you must be willing to drop other concerns to respond. For Suzy and Arlene, one day was particularly critical. Suzy could easily have put off her phone calls for a day or two, but then it might have been too late—too late to demonstrate to her mother how much she cared for her.

Of course, Arlene's loss was obvious. The losses that first shock older people are often such medical events—a stroke, a heart attack, a flu that the elder can't shake. In others, the sense of loss may be triggered by a social event: An older woman looks around at a party and realizes that her two best friends have died. Or another close friend moves away and into a retirement center. Again, the loss may be purely internal—a depression born of the reduction of inner vitality.

Family members should be alert for any of these signs— not merely to be able to help during the immediate crisis, but because their first response sets the pattern for the future. If the first shock of loss draws the generations together, if it brings out greater frankness and greater tenderness, then very likely subsequent losses will bring increasing intimacy. On the other hand, if the generations seem out of synchronization and the need can't be matched by appropriate concern, parents and children can develop an enduring apartness.

Divorced when her youngest daughter Nancy was five, Margaret never remarried. Nor did she seem to want to, though she was the only divorced person in their small midwestern town.

Margaret developed a tough hide, became more "manly." She worked for the power company, did well, and gave her three daughters the kind of upbringing she thought they needed. But Margaret was not one to give verbal praise, and she wasn't a "hugger" by nature. Nancy, in particular, suffered as "the stupid one." Margaret had thought calling her stupid would motivate her to excel.

The three girls grew up, married and had children. Out of duty they kept in touch with their mother, though none of them felt close to her. When Nancy's second child was three months old, Nancy made a trip to visit

Margaret. One morning during her stay, they found the child dead in his crib. His death was diagnosed as SIDS—Sudden Infant Death Syndrome.

Six months later Nancy had a breakdown, accompanied by loss of weight and emotional instability. Soon after, her husband asked for a divorce. Fortunately, however, with the help of some friends and a counselor, they were able to reconcile.

Through the haze of depression, Nancy gradually became aware that her mother was also having a difficult time. Margaret felt extremely guilty over the child's death, imagining that she hadn't taken enough time for him, that she hadn't picked him up and held him. She also felt the weight of her daughter's emotional problems, and began to hint that she blamed herself for them. Margaret had never allowed herself the luxury of introspection, but now she began reviewing her life as a parent. Margaret—strong, confident Margaret—began to focus solely on what was wrong with her.

When Nancy realized that her mother was blaming herself, her perception of her mother changed. Nancy began to realize how difficult life as a single parent must have been for Margaret.

Nancy began to write letters expressing thanks for her mother's parenting. Seeking to put her mother's failings into perspective, she commended her mother for holding the family together and teaching them all responsibility. Margaret responded to her daughter's reassurance, and a new warmth developed between them.

Doubting What You've Done

The last thing Nancy expected was for her mother to begin doubting herself. Yet older people often wonder whether their lives have been worth anything. While you might not be surprised to learn that people who never "amounted to much" question their worth, the same searching evaluation often comes to people whose achievements seem enviable. For example:

"You suppose that I contemplate my life's work with calm satisfaction. But seen close the whole thing has quite a different look. There is not one single notion that I am convinced will hold its ground and broadly speaking I am not certain of being on the right path. Our contemporaries look upon me both as a heretic and as a reactionary who has, as it were, outlived himself. To be sure, this is a question of fashion and of a short-sighted view; but the feeling of inadequacy comes from within."—Albert Einstein

"Life is a long preparation for something that never happens."—William Butler Yeats.

"So now, from this mad passion
Which made me take art for an idol and a king
I have learnt the burden of error that it bore
And what misfortune springs from man's desire . . .
The world's frivolities have robbed me of the time
That I was given for reflecting upon God."
—Michelangelo

"The heart does not grow old, but it is sad to dwell among ruins."—Voltaire.

"The change is not perhaps very obvious; everything is still as interesting as it was and qualities have not undergone important modifications either; but something in the nature of a resonance is lacking. I am no musician, yet here I feel the same difference that there is when one presses on the pedal or when one does not."—Sigmund Freud

One could add almost indefinitely to this list of quotations from famous older people. Melancholy, wistfulness, philosophy—they are common among many older people. So are peacefulness, meditation, prayerfulness among older believers. Research indicates a general shift from action toward reflection.

Creativity need not die. Goethe was over 80 when he completed *Faust*. Michelangelo, despite his doubts about the value of art, did some of his best work as an old man; he completed the dome of St. Peter's at the age of 70. Nobel Prize–winning author Francois Mauriac explained the origin of his final novel this way: "On my eightieth birthday, I said to myself, 'Since I seem to be a long way from dying, why not write another novel?'" It was a best-seller. Yet the offhand manner of expression is notable: "Why not?" rather than, "I must!"

It reflects an internal change of the weather. Mauriac put it this way: "I do not feel detached from anyone or any thing. But from now on living will be enough to keep me occupied. This blood which still flows in the hand I lay upon my knee . . . this transitory, not eternal ebb and flow, this world so close to its end—all these insist upon being watched every moment, all these last moments before the very last: that is what old age is. . . . I should like to think of nothing at all except that I exist and that I am here."

Another aging Christian is quoted by writer Ronald Blythe as saying, "I care less. I feel now that I am tempted to hand everything over to God and to leave it at that. I don't really care two hoots about lots of things now. They make no impact on me at all."

A friend of mine, Dorothy Becker, put it more positively: "When you're raising a family and trying to make a living, you don't have much time to think about what you should strive for. There isn't time to think about why am I here, what are my objectives. You have to live right for the present. But since I retired, I've had time to sit down and write down my thoughts. I write a lot of verse, just corny stuff. It's nothing that could be published, but my family loves it. That's one of the nice things about retirement years. You can sit in front of your window and watch the sun set on a mountain. You can sit and just think about the beautiful things in life, and you know you won't have to jump up and run to get a meal on. I have just loved retirement, and I've said umpteen times, I wish I'd done it sooner."

Reflection may be melancholic, but need not be. Ronald Blythe quotes one elderly man this way: "Everybody screams—and I include myself—'I can't do this and I can't do that!' and 'I used to do this and I used to do that!' and 'Baaah!' The lesson to be learnt is to understand the promotion from plum-easy doing to the surprisingly difficult non-activity of just being. Be patient, be gentle, be nothing. Somebody said that the real vocation of old age was to give out love."

From Solitude to Dialogue

If reflection is to be fruitful and lead to growth, elders need to bring their thoughts out of solitude and into some kind of dialogue. Margaret needed to talk to Nancy.

Alone, elders often reach an impasse in their thoughts, or go in circles. How can they break new ground? Elders may share with peers, or with a husband or wife, or even with a grandchild. They may express their struggles through a journal, or on canvas. But very often parents and their children must be the principal dialogue partners of the Second Day, simply because their relationship deepens so much more significantly as the week goes on.

Perhaps more than at any other time of life, parents and their children share parallel concerns. These concerns, if understood, can form the basis for deep, empathetic sharing.

In *Aging is a Family Affair*, Bumagin and Hirn draw some of these parallel concerns between the older and middle generations:

Middlers: How can I get my children/parents to listen to me?
Elders: Who listens to old people?

Middlers: How can I balance all my responsibilities?
Elders: Who will take care of me?

Middlers: How can I have a life of my own?
Elders: How can I stay independent?

Middlers: How can I do something meaningful with my life while there is still time?
Elders: How can I continue to be myself despite all these changes?

Middlers: How can I stop feeling guilty?
Elders: What has my life been worth?

Middlers: How can I shed the dread of knowing that Mother/Father might die soon?
Elders: Will I be ready when my time comes?

People often wish they could express such concerns, but find it difficult to know how to begin. They may hint about their feelings, hoping that a parent (or child) will ask further questions. They may long for, and perhaps periodically try for, a "breakthrough" conversation. But breakthroughs rarely occur in just one session. Empathetic communication normally builds up over the course of time, bit by bit. That is where the art of visiting comes in.

Asking Good Questions

Gradually, incrementally, "visiting" becomes the chief mode of interaction between parents and children. Through most of life, parents and their children meet through events. A birthday party, a trip, a holiday, or a chore bring the generations together. In old age, however, this pattern begins to change. Events continue, of course, but "visits" increase as parents become less active.

Aging mothers don't prepare meals for twelve any more, so the family doesn't celebrate Thanksgiving at the family home. Older parents may stop driving, so transporting them to another house for a birthday party becomes a significant chore. Over time, the activities that created many fond memories—cooking and eating and cleaning up after meals, opening presents, shopping, going for a walk—tend to diminish. The number of people present dwindles to a few. Without an event, and without numbers of people, parents and children are confronted by blocks of empty time.

Unfortunately, many parents and children have managed to go through life without learning how to carry on a decent conversation. They bog down in small talk, not knowing how to ask the kinds of questions that probe important issues and ideas. They need to learn a new skill.

Good visiting is essentially the same in the hospital or at home, and indeed, on the telephone. Visiting is largely the art of good listening—listening that facilitates conversation. A woman told Ronald Blythe, "One of the worst things about being eighty is the constant foolish chat, the patronizing little sayings which keep on coming your way." Good visiting doesn't stoop to that level.

What can children—or any visitor—ask about? A prime topic is the elder's past life. Many elders are both interested and interesting on the subject. Some, though, repeat a few well-rehearsed stories. Here is a brief sampler of questions one may ask to get at fresher memories—and perhaps stimulate an older person to think about his past from a different angle:

- What house do you remember best from childhood?
- What was church like during your childhood?
- Did you have a favorite teacher in elementary school? In high school?
- What kind of marriage did your mother and father have? How did they affect your thinking about marriage?
- How would you describe your feelings during WWII?
- Tell me about your boyfriends/girlfriends when you were a young woman/man.
- What music do you remember most vividly?
- When you were young, what did you think old age would be like?

The elderly, I have found, are more likely than younger people to rise to a tough question. They aren't likely to blurt out an answer, but take time to consider it carefully. If they have entered the Second Day, reflection is a more natural mode for them. Yet they need someone to ask the question, and listen to the answer, and explore further meaning. Some elders like to air their thoughts on the meaning of life, on politics, or on religion. Here is a brief sampler of more philosophically oriented questions:

- What should a person in his twenties/thirties/forties/fifties concentrate on doing with his life?
- Is life really any different today than it was fifty years ago?
- Who do you think was the best president of the United States in your lifetime?
- What do you think is the most important quality a man/woman can show toward his/her wife/husband?
- Would another Depression be good for this country?

It's extremely interesting for adult children to ask their parents about themselves as children. For example:

- How did you see me acting differently from my siblings?
- Did I ever do anything that really hurt you? Worried you?

- Did you ever feel guilty for something you did to one of us children?
- How would you describe yourself as a parent?
- What for you was the happiest Christmas we spent as a family?

A family photo album can be a wonderful tool for stimulating conversation, as you get a parent to describe your relatives or to recount past events. (You might want a tape recorder around for some of this.) You can also use magazines, newspapers or library books to promote discussion about historical events.

The Art of Visiting

A visitor represents a wider world of activity and vitality that an older person fears being cut off from. So, when you visit, in addition to questions, bring news of family, friends, and church; bring a child along, or a friend. Make a point of stating your thoughts and feelings. Ask advice, if you can ask sincerely.

The frankness with which elders can express their doubts, their fears, their cynicism, may be alarming. I think of one old man who looked me in the eye. "When you've lived as long as I have," he said, "you'll realize that a man past 60 isn't worth a plugged nickel. They should just take you out and shoot you."

Some grow more dogmatic with the years; others begin to openly speculate about beliefs they have held all their lives. An elder may upset her family by wondering openly whether there really is a God. Or, an elder may allow repressed racism to surface.

An older person has little to lose in saying exactly what she thinks. Sometimes an elder will say something shocking in order to gain attention, or to break out of the "nice old lady" stereotype. Older people often feel nobody listens to them, and some wild statement can put the listener to the test. Younger people who find this worrisome or depressing will want to change the tone of the conversation. But they cannot succeed in force-feeding good cheer; worries will surface, in one way or another.

It is not necessary to agree with what is said, or to let it go unchallenged, but it is always necessary to respect the person saying it. It helps to remember what an older person is facing. The elderly, like the rest of us, need to vent their concerns in order to work them through. All that is required is an attentive and sympathetic ear.

It is usually wise to make visits as routine as clockwork. Regularly scheduled visits allow the older person the joy of anticipation, as well as the joy of the visit itself. I have known older people who oriented the better part of a day around one, brief, anticipated visit. If they don't know when you're coming, their thoughts are more likely to be anxious: "Will she ever come?"

For long-distance "visiting," routine also helps. Write or call on schedule if possible. One advantage of a letter over a call is that a letter can be read and reread. Tape recordings are another alternative, particularly for a parent whose eyes are failing or one who does not enjoy reading. A recording need not be long, and can be played time and again. Send clippings, snapshots, magazines. All these enlarge the elder's world.

The most important thing you have to offer, nonetheless, is yourself. That is to say, you offer not merely your physical presence, but your attentive love, your concern, your empathy. It is better to give this fully for ten minutes than to visit too long and give only divided or halfhearted attention.

A bored, nervous, dutiful visitor conveys a clear message to an older person. Try to be fully there, body and soul. When you lack the patience for that, experiment with shorter visits, or vary the visits with some activity—a walk, a reading, a drive, a game.

> "Young people often say, 'Would you like to be young again,' and don't really like it when you say no. I soften the blow. I say, 'Just think of all the years I should have been done out of heaven.' Though that doesn't please them much either. When you are young, you think it is better to be young than in heaven. . . .
>
> "The action is over, so far as I am concerned, but I hope that, now I am an old man, there is something written into me, or on me—an epistle which people who encounter me can read. I mean, I hope that what I've done has left some sort of mark. . . . Old men are heavily marked and can be read. Good things, bad things, are in their marks."
>
> Quoted in Ronald Blythe's *A View in Winter.*

Life Review

When older people enter the Second Day, many gain a far clearer memory of their childhood years. They can sometimes hear the voices of childhood friends, see their faces, remember places and events and smells and colors in a way they have not been able to for years. Some of these memories are delightful. Some are painful. The people elders have hurt come back to mind; they may remember the words, the facial expressions. Small-child feelings of guilt and lostness seem fresh. So does the heart-stopping love of a mother, now gone. So does the summer twilight. Older people sometimes linger in this treasure house.

Older people will also review their adult lives: accomplishments and failures in their jobs, their families, their lives with God, their marriages. They will think with satisfaction or despair of things done and left undone.

It is no wonder, then, that some elderly people "live in the past." They lose interest in the present, compared to their fascination for rehearsing events long gone. Younger people—and even elderly peers—often grow impatient with this, sensing that memories can be used to keep the present at a distance.

On the other hand, older people may become attached to old photos, to old stories, and to other artifacts from their past for positive reasons. In the rush of drastic personal change, they are seeking to hold on to their identity. That is not living in the past; it is self-protection in the present. But if elders are to continue to grow in their old age—and they need to grow, to face the challenges aging will bring— then protecting their past identity is not enough. Elders must come to terms with the past, yet not become lost in it. They must "find themselves"—their present selves. This is what "life review" therapy is designed to do.

"Life review" can be accomplished through various techniques such as encouraging a senior to write an autobiography, tell his life story aloud, maybe even to illustrate the past—say, drawing pictures of all the houses he has ever lived in. Photographs can be used to spur memories. Frequently, educational programs designed for seniors include a "life review" workshop—usually a group of older people meeting to encourage each other through the process.

Other people, particularly relatives, will probably be interested in the memoirs, and this interest is often what inspires an older person to go to the trouble of writing them down. They want to record some family history for the grandchildren, and thus to leave a part of themselves behind. Life review, though, is not best understood as a history project. It is a religious process, a search through the memories for the person who lived this life—an attempt at a fuller understanding of oneself. The procedure provides a structure for meditating on the past in order to *harvest* the past.

Life review attempts to understand the past but its interest is finally in the present; indeed, the future. It seeks to answer these questions: In all my relationships and roles, lived throughout these 70 or more years, what message has been written into my life? Who am I, and who am I at my best? Who do I want to be? What have I done that satisfies me, and what now seems insignificant? What can my successes and failures teach me about life? What in the final analysis has God had to say to me and about me?

Prayers for "healing of the memories" often do something similar. Calling up memories of their past (often with the help of a trained leader), people imagine Jesus' presence with them through their experiences. They want to understand—not just intellectually but emotionally—Jesus in his relation to them throughout their life. This kind of healing prayer, valuable at any age, may be particularly apt in the Second Day.

If God Is For Us

Sometimes remembering is sad or bitter. It would be easier to drift in a nostalgic haze, avoiding some of the painful aspects of the past. But even melancholy thoughts are essential. An older person must come to grips with his losses and failures, and then come to grips with the larger fact of God's power, his understanding, and his forgiveness. "If God is for us, who can be against us? He who did not spare his own Son, but gave him up for us all—how will he not also, along with him, graciously give us all things?

Who will bring any charge against those whom God has chosen? It is God who justifies. Who is he that condemns?" (Rom. 8:31–34).

An older person considering his past will certainly find reason for regret. Yet this exploration should carry him beyond regret, to the point of saying, with Christ, "Not guilty!" With that verdict on the past, the future looks hopeful. "Will he not also . . . graciously give us all things?"

Elders who accept Jesus' forgiveness may learn to echo Paul: "Whatever was to my profit I now consider loss for the sake of Christ. What is more, I consider everything a loss compared to the surpassing greatness of knowing Christ Jesus my Lord, for whose sake I have lost all things. I consider them rubbish, that I may gain Christ and be found in him" (Phil. 3:7–9).

This shift of values, which Paul considered essential to the Christian life, is particularly thrust on old people. A Catholic priest, Father Congreve, wrote as an old man: "If I find no home any longer in this world, it is because God has been withdrawing me, my love, my treasures, my re-membrances, my hopes, from a place where the frost-wind of death touched every precious thing, where no good can last, but night falls, and only icy solitude and silence re-main. This is no home, this is but a lodging. . . . God is making all things dark and silent around me. . . . I must begin to long for home."—*Life Preview*

An older person tends, somewhat naturally, to ponder what purpose his life has served. That is good, but it is not enough. He or she needs to shift to thoughts of what purpose life yet holds.

Along with life review, older people need life *preview*. Drawing on lifelong experience, they should confront the future. "If given two more years, or twenty, what do I want to do with my life?" these elders should ask. "What story should these remaining years tell my children and grandchildren? As an old tree, what new shoots do I hope to produce?"

Maud Royden put it this way: "They say we are going downhill—but they are wrong. We are going *up*hill, which is why it is such heavy going!"

For a materialist who measures life in terms of what he can do and what pleasure he receives, the losses of old age can be absolutely devastating. The best he can do is hold his losses at bay, and squeeze a little dying pleasure out of whatever time is left. I heard recently, for instance, of an older couple who were traveling for all they were worth, trying to see as many sights as possible before the wife, who was slowly losing her sight, became completely blind.

I don't fault them for that. But one needs more to base the future on. When the blindness comes, I hope the sights they have seen contribute to a sense of warmth, shared joy, and accomplishment. I hope that the sights were more than a last fling as the sun sets.

A Christian must ultimately count on another reality, defined by Jesus when he walked resolutely toward suffering and death. He "resolutely set out for Jerusalem" (Luke 9:51). We honor him as the great, living Ruler of the world, not because he won great honors or did great things, not because he healed thousands and influenced millions, but because he faced death and conquered it on our behalf. Now we all must choose whether or not to take his life as the prime example for ours.

Earlier in life this question may have seemed abstract. But in the Second Day its realism becomes apparent. Those living in the Day of Reflection ought ideally to reflect on this. And many elders do. Though it is not by any means guaranteed that elders will grow "more religious," there are many who find themselves drawn into a deeper life of seeking God.

Practical Preparations in the Second Day

The Second Day sounds an alarm, changing an older person's sense of what the future holds. This is the time for reflection and preparation. I have concentrated on spiritual reflection and preparation, for I think it is central. But there are other important ways to get ready.

Wills, powers of attorney, lists, doctors. In the last chapter (pp. 72–81) I described the preparations for death that ought to be made early in retirement. In fact, very few elders make these preparations, because they haven't accepted the fact that they will grow old and die. When they begin to face losses in the Second Day, however, they may be persuaded that these preparations are truly worthwhile.

Health concerns assume a new urgency. A person enjoying retired life in the First Day is not very likely to want to change a lifetime habit of enjoying potato chips. But after a mild heart attack brought on by high blood pressure, he is much more likely to be receptive to his doctor's warnings.

Gerontologists report that health problems in older people are often caused by or made worse by malnutrition. Solitude, sickness, fatigue and a diminishing sense of taste can lead older people to eat junk food in preference for cooking regular meals. An older person may be gaining weight, but not getting enough protein, for instance. Good eating habits, developed now, can be extremely helpful later, when losses mount up. Community dining rooms (available to seniors in many communities, and always offering balanced meals) can literally help to prolong life.

Smoking, alcohol, and other drugs add strain to an increasingly fragile constitution. It is never too late to quit.

Studies show that moderate, regular exercise can be extremely helpful in old age. Exercise helps to control weight gain, and seems to have a significant tranquilizing effect on older people.

A great many older people need to watch their blood pressure. Diet, exercise and medication can help a great deal. The incidence of strokes in older people has dropped dramatically, largely due to the way doctors have helped people monitor their blood pressure. The careful habits that are required, however, ideally start before there is a great health risk.

Social concerns in the later years also require preparation. Older people need relationships that can support them during times of loss. They may find those friends within their family, or in church, neighborhood, or voluntary organizations. Often the relationships already exist, but need cultivation. For instance, seniors are usually in touch with their children, but they may never have developed good communication with them. They may be members of a church, but may not have committed themselves to strong involvement and mutual support.

Most people do not find it easy to make friends when they are past 30, let alone when they are past 70. I have been particularly impressed that my father-in-law, though hardly a social butterfly, has continued making new and very close friends into his seventies. I have also been impressed by the number of his close friends who have died. When losses begin to hit, many older people need particular encouragement to widen their circle and cultivate new friendships. Men, in particular, need this help; they seem often to have few friends, and rely heavily on the sociability of their wives.

Role concerns have to do with the probable death of the

spouse. Nothing can really prepare a person for this devastating loss of companionship. It is possible, however, to prepare for the loss of the skills that a spouse tends to specialize in.

Lynn Caine, in her book *Widows*, suggests a yearly "contingency day" in which couples talk about and rehearse the strategies that would be called for in case of death. What financial moves should be made? Who should be contacted? For instance, the person who doesn't have the responsibility for paying the bills in the family should do it once, under the direction of the spouse who normally handles the finances.

Another strategic necessity is "home survival." In most cases, the husband will be the "innocent party"—innocent of competence. Making beds with hospital corners is definitely not essential. But knowing how to cook two or three decent meals is. Cleaning the bathroom, running the dishwasher, doing laundry, paying bills, and repairing leaky faucets—these skills seem obvious to someone who does them regularly, but can be extraordinarily difficult for someone who has never made them a priority. It's important to learn these skills *before* the crisis. Otherwise, completing these tasks alone for the first time can reinforce a cycle of depression for a man or woman who is grieving a lost spouse.

DAY 3

MEMO TO MY MOTHER:

BEFORE NOW I NEVER THOUGHT MUCH ABOUT
*it when I heard that an older person had lost a spouse. A child
dying of leukemia shakes me; but the end of forty or fifty years
of loving, daily companionship I have treated as something
ordinary.*

*I have been powerfully affected by my conversations with
widows. The impact of their loss is so plainly overwhelming.
These conversations have made me think of you. It is extremely
hard to imagine, and indeed I do not want to imagine it: We
will probably attend, together, Dad's funeral. I try to think of
this, and I see scenes out of a movie, with flowers and black-
clad pallbearers, but I do not really see us. I suppose what they
say is true: To a child, parents are immortal. Until they die.*

*It is equally hard to imagine what it would mean for you to
be alone, without Dad. You have given your life to him. You
have laughed at, and struggled with, his oddness. You have loved
him patiently and forcefully, and you have been loved in return.*

Together you have made the innumerable fine adjustments necessary to a marriage between two strong individuals. The fact that all of us kids have managed strong, happy marriages is a tribute to your example.

Yet your partnership will end. I know that, though I cannot quite imagine it. It will be as though, one old intertwined tree having fallen, the other's shape is seen clearly for the first time.

The Third Day:
Losing a Spouse

HOWARD TOOK HIS WIFE, MARGE, TO THE HOS-
pital for a routine biopsy. She never left. This is what
Howard says:

"When I took her in there she was, to all intents and
purposes, a well woman with a sore throat. And she was
in intensive care for 51 days. Never spoke to me another
word from the time she went in till the time she came out.
She had a tube down her throat with a rubber guard over
the tube so she couldn't bite it through.

"I was with her every day. They let me in the intensive
care room with her. I didn't bother anybody, just sat in the
corner and watched her. She knew I was there, though she
couldn't see me. She couldn't wear her glasses, couldn't
talk to me.

"I was reassured constantly that she was getting better.
If they hoped she was going to get stronger and get well,
why didn't they start the chemotherapy and physical ther-

apy? Why did they wait until the last week? They had some strong young Swedish woman from the therapist department upstairs come down, and they put an aluminum plate at the foot of her bed to strengthen her legs and her feet.

"Then three nurses would get her on her feet and walk her around the room in the walker. They had a portable oxygen mask on her face and tried to get her to shuffle along from the bed to the chair and back to the bed again. And what a big, big deal it was. Oh, how they thought that was a big deal to show me that she was getting along. And then they brought in these different specialists, putting drops in her hands and trying to inject fluid into her veins to give her relief. I have nothing against these kids, they were trying to do what they could. One girl was trying so hard. She tried so hard.

"I slammed my hand down. 'Leave her alone! What are you trying to do!' She was a guinea pig. And she had written a note: 'Get me out of this! Get me out of this!'

"Well, you've got to have faith in God. You've got to take God's word for it that his will is being worked in these cases, not the will of man. But why does the doctor have to lie about it? Why doesn't he come out and tell you, 'Mr. Smith, I can't do a darn thing for your wife.' Why doesn't he tell you after 10 days instead of waiting 51 days? Why can't he tell you that right off the bat? If people would just tell the truth and stop kidding old people. They think because we're old, we're senile.

"I had no bad feelings about her dying. It's just that she had to lie there and suffer for so long. But after I got out of the hospital and after she passed away, it didn't seem to bother me as much.

"If I could just go in a corner someplace and kick up my heels and cry my fool head off I'd feel a lot better, but I can't do it. I couldn't when my first wife died. I cannot stand off in a corner someplace and cry like a baby. I wish I could.

"Well, the first year is pretty rough and the second year is pretty rough. The moment you lose somebody, you have friends galore. They come in, the offers of food and help and everything else are fantastic. But, three weeks after, the offers stop. You're again left alone. You're the third wheel on the cart. They don't need you.

"It's hard to live alone. It's harder for a man than a woman. I've got a hobby, messing around in the shed out there. I could take you out and show it to you and in five minutes' time, it's all over. Your wife can talk about the children, she can talk about hemlining a dress, or she can talk about anything that comes into her mind. Lots of women talk and they can keep talking. They can make friends, where you and I would have one heck of a job making friends."

Grief Work

You can hear the desolation in Howard's voice. The medical establishment is only a convenient target for his anger. He has lost the one person for whom he was, without reservation, of first importance. He has lost his best companion, who by her sociability made it easier for him to live in the world. Nothing—not his children, not his hobby—can replace her. He is staggering from the hurt. At whom can he scream?

It would seem that Howard had a happy marriage. But the happily married are not the only ones who grieve. Studies indicate that difficult marriages may actually be harder to mourn. When a happy marriage ends, the grief is straightforward. When a difficult marriage ends, grief is mixed with guilt and regret. All married couples adjust their lives to each other; even in unhappiness they achieve a certain stability. When one partner dies, that stability is shattered. A junkpile of hurts and unfulfilled wishes and unforgiven flaws is hard to sort and put away into the past.

Initially, of course, friends expect (and possibly dread) some demonstrations of grief, but within a few weeks or months they begin to feel, "This has gone on long enough." They want mourners to "get over it," to "cheer up." Yet as Bumagin and Hirn write, "The grief work following a death can no more be successfully avoided than the labor pains preceding a birth." Mourners have to go through it. Those who are a picture of serenity at the funeral may grieve less obviously, and the loss may not hit them until months later, but they too will grieve.

Grief this heavy wants out. Howard would give anything to stand in a corner and bawl, but he cannot: the grief plugs him up. Those who can cry feel as though their intestines are pulled up and out, and yet always there is more of that sick feeling inside. The comforters will want to make the hurt go away, but no one can do that. Comforters should simply listen and demonstrate love, keeping the mourner company all they can, or all he wants.

Comments intended to point out the silver lining in the cloud, such as, "Isn't it a blessing he didn't suffer?" should not be pressed. They tend to repress grief when what the grieving person needs is a way to express it. When a grieving person is ready to see the bright side, he or she will usually let you know.

Typically, as Howard indicated, friends are very responsive during the first three weeks. Yet this is the least difficult period. The grieving spouse is occupied with the busy work that accompanies death: arranging the funeral and burial, informing insurance companies and other legal entities, sorting possessions. Only after life has settled back to normal does the depth of loss sink in. Two years is a good estimate of the length of time a spouse is likely to be preoccupied with grief—to be aware of the absence of the loved one every single day.

Family members—children, particularly—and close friends should try to maintain as much contact as possible during this whole period. Their caring contact may save a life. A study in Wales showed that in the first year of grieving, close relatives of the deceased were seven times more likely to die than the general population. Widowers were *ten* times more likely to die. By the second year, the ratio decreased, though it was still formidable—the bereaved were not quite twice as likely to die.

Perhaps the best help a grieving spouse can find is from another widow or widower. Having already made the transition to a new life, he or she can speak with authority to the bereaved person. Some communities have voluntary organizations designed to link widows together for just this purpose. And almost any church is likely to have widows who would welcome an invitation to give special care to someone who has recently lost a spouse.

Family members should be particularly aware of holidays—Christmas, Thanksgiving and Easter, wedding anniversaries, birthdays, anniversaries of the death—for these are times when grief commonly surfaces. People usually try to keep the sadness at bay, not to give in to it. But it would be better to allow for time to be sad, to acknowledge the absence of a loved one, to say how much you miss her. It also helps to try observing the holidays in a slightly different way. Go to a different home. Attend a new church service.

Vary the dinner menu. Adding something new to your habitual celebration says, symbolically, that life still offers new possibilities.

Mildred and her husband Jerry had moved to a new town about a year and a half before Jerry, a heavy smoker, became sick. He was in and out of the hospital for several months. About a week after being released, he and Mildred were alone at home one night. He spasmed, choked, collapsed. Mildred, a nurse, held him and practiced mouth-to-mouth resuscitation. "I knew it wasn't going to do any good," she says, but for some time she worked over him, breathing her air into his lungs.

After the funeral, Mildred took a week off work and then tried to return to her normal routine. Since Jerry, a drug salesman, had always traveled during the week, she was used to being alone. And Mildred is not one to allow herself self-pity.

Yet when the family had gone, she was faced with terrible loneliness. She went to church on Sunday, but had to get out of the building because of the memories of Jerry's memorial service, held in the sanctuary. Usually, though, the emptiness was discovered in more incidental ways. "I would see a certain kind of car coming down the street and I'd say, 'Oh, there's Jerry.'" Then the truth would close in, that she would never again see her loved one drive up.

About six weeks after Jerry's death, Mildred reached her lowest point. She felt she had to talk to someone, and went to see her doctor. He listened and gave her a speech about getting up and building a new life for herself. "Nobody is going to like you if you're down in the mouth all the time." He urged her to go out and make new friends.

The timing was right. She and her husband had always played bridge and golf together, but as a widow she didn't feel that she fit into the old groups. She didn't much try. Her doctor's encouragement set her in new directions. She made friends at church, and became involved in Bible study for the first time in her life. Another widow invited her along on several trips. Mildred also moved from her duplex, which was too full of Jerry, into a new mobile home.

Nevertheless, though she appeared to be doing well, the feelings of loneliness continued. "It took three to five years to really get my bearings again. There are still times after fifteen years when I would give anything in the world to reach out and touch him. You do miss male companionship."

The Most Devastating Loss?

Getting old involves many losses, often intertwined and overlapping. The loss of a spouse, however, stands on its own, simply because it overwhelms other losses. I call it the Third Day in the week of old age, though chronologically it can come at any point.

If I am typical of younger people, we think more of other old-age losses. Perhaps marriage, with its foundation of passion, does not fit with our image of age. Nonetheless, when you talk to elderly people about their experiences, the loss of a spouse stands out. People often describe their lives in terms of a great historical event: "Those were the Depression years," or "That was during Vietnam." Widows say, as though it explains everything, "That was the year Jerry died."

Since most people (more than four out of five) reach the age of 65 still married, and since a married pair rarely die at the same time, the death of a spouse is a reality awaiting a very large proportion of older people—and awaiting most women. Women live about seven years longer than men, and are on average four years younger than their husbands, so women are left alone for an average of 11 full years. Eleven years—enough time for a younger woman to leave college and become a respected veteran in her profession, while marrying and becoming the mother of three well-spaced children.

For women aged 65 to 74 (the young old), over 40 percent are widows. Beyond 75, nearly 70 percent are widows. For men, the corresponding percentages are 10 percent and 21 percent.

Men do not, on the whole, adjust well to being left alone. Without a wife, many are unable to cope with keeping a house and cooking. More troublesome is the common male inability to socialize. Their loneliness is an unsolvable riddle, if they have not learned to make friends. Many remarry; they know no other way to solve their loneliness. (Since single women so outnumber single men in these later years, women are less likely to have this option.)

For women, too, losing a spouse means great loneliness. They may have other friends, even better friends than their husband, but not one to whom they have been so bonded. A spouse takes up a huge place in their lives, filling it in a way for which friends cannot substitute.

Many widows (and widowers) report an eerie sense that their lost love is still present. They turn around, thinking he is there. They "feel" his presence. But this feeling is not comforting. It is no substitute for the flesh they have loved so many years. This is one major reason why widows and widowers often want to move to a new home.

One woman and her husband had always watched football together. After he died she sat in front of the television and watched, out of habit, nearly a whole season of football alone. Once she turned to say something to him, and stopped when she saw his empty chair. Eventually she realized that she did not really like football; she liked his company.

Most widows feel they must drop out of the society of couples they have enjoyed with their husband. They feel naked without an escort at social affairs. A retired man told me recently of driving several widows home from a church function. Another older woman had brought her husband to the dinner, even though he was in such bad physical condition she had to feed him like a child. My retired friend overheard the conversation of the other women who had lost their own husbands and were openly envious of the woman who still had hers. "I just couldn't believe my ears!" he said.

The loneliness is sexual as well as social. In shocking contradiction to our childhood sense of what parents (let alone grandparents) are like, all available data show that unless illness makes it impossible, sexual activity can and often does continue into the eighties and nineties. For instance, one study found that 70 percent of married men aged 70 were sexually active, having intercourse about once a week. (Upon reading this, a friend in his thirties exclaimed, "So it'll increase!") Losing this intimate contact, with all it means for one's sense of being valued, loved and nurtured, leaves a large and unmentionable gap.

The Practical Needs of a Widow

A widow (or widower) also faces huge practical difficulties. She is likely to have expended enormous amounts of energy in caring for her spouse through an extended illness; therefore, she will begin her grieving totally exhausted. Then she must do all kinds of unfamiliar tasks—tasks necessary in dealing with dying, such as choosing a casket; and tasks the loved one has always done, such as determining whether that rattling noise in the front of the car represents danger to life and limb.

On top of that, a widow's financial situation is likely to be worse than it was when her husband was alive. Her

Social Security check will probably decrease, especially if she did not work extensively outside the home. Pensions may be similarly reduced or ended.

Put together, these factors create tremendous emotional and physical strain. Yet, since the obvious crisis seems to have ended with the death of her spouse, widows are easily forgotten.

From the Bible's fundamental concern for justice comes its persistent concern for widows. In a patriarchal society, lacking a male to protect them, they could easily be abused. Since there is no man to take their part, God takes their part, and the protection of their rights (along with those of other defenseless people) becomes almost a formula in Scripture: "Do not take advantage of a widow or an orphan," God warns. "If you do and they cry out to me, I will certainly hear their cry" (Exod. 22:22–23).

Yet the needs of widows continued. In the first-century Jerusalem church, widows had to depend on church handouts for survival, and disputes arose over fair treatment. (See Acts 6:1.) The problem was again addressed when Paul wrote to Timothy, devoting considerable space to instructions about the care of widows. He expected the church to provide help, yet stressed the family's primary responsibility. "If anyone does not provide for his relatives, and especially for his immediate family, he has denied the faith and is worse than an unbeliever" (1 Tim. 5:8).

That comment still stands. We have more elderly widows than ever before. They are often poor. But their economic needs may be their smallest problem. They do not fit into a family-oriented society, and often their grief has taken away the strength they need to break out of isolation. In their loneliness, they have great needs for support and companionship. If I am right in calling the loss of a spouse the hardest blow an older person can face, then church and society—and particularly family—ought to be more conscious of it. The Bible calls us to be.

Kaye is in her nineties. She has been a widow for forty years, since her husband's heart gave out after years of illness.

Fortunately, her husband left her with a home. (Doctor bills had eaten up virtually all their savings.) But she could not bear to stay in it. Her husband had been a civic leader in their small town, and without him all her social status had vanished. She felt restless and unhappy. Grown children lived in other states, and so she began to travel to see them. "I counted up once that I traveled more than a dozen times across the U.S. I seemed to want to be on the move. I was lonely and didn't want to face life alone."

Travel didn't help. She lost weight until she was little more than skin and bones. Her father died a year after her husband, and so did her sister's husband. Kaye kept moving, restlessly. She realized what she was doing, but couldn't stop. Looking back now, she thinks there was nothing anyone could have done to help. She had to come to terms with aloneness on her own. "My daughter and son were very kind to let me stay with them. But finally I saw that they couldn't have a normal life, and neither could I."

Two years after her husband died, Kaye was ready to move on with life. She settled back into her home, this time for good. Her friendship with a woman at church began to blossom. "Barbara and I were two lonely people who needed each other. I loved her from the start, and evidently she felt the same. She has been my closest friend for 25 years. She knows things about my family that no one else knows. My life would have been so empty without her. We confide in each other. She's always been available."

Kaye wrote me a note when she read my summary of our conversation describing these years. "I feel that I have come a long way from that wimpy woman," she says. "To God be the glory."

New Possibilities

A widow's life is not all sadness, for rising out of the depths of loss can be new growth. While the grieving continues, these possibilities seem remote; it would be cruel even to mention them. Later, though, when the mourning has begun to spend itself, a widow begins to ask, "What next?"

A widow who has spent her life bending to the personality of a partner can now explore her own likes and dislikes. She is, as Paul indicates in Scripture, freer to develop her life with God. (See 1 Cor. 7:8, 32–35; 1 Tim. 5:5.) She is freer to strengthen friendships with her children and with others outside the family. She may be freer from responsibilities, freer to travel, freer to try new activities. One need not depreciate the marriage to believe that, when the marriage is ended by death, new and positive possibilities arise. Sometimes family members and friends discover a man or woman whose character they barely knew before the death of the spouse.

Often, these new possibilities are like those of the First Day—Freedom Day. At least the questions ought to be framed in the same way: "With the time God gives me, and in these new circumstances of my life, what am I called to do and to be?" The answers will be as varied as those given to the same question after retirement. Some widows will volunteer for challenging new jobs. Some will concentrate on caring for grandchildren and children. Some will give themselves to friendships and Bible study, as Kaye did. Some will find joy in art, or pleasure, or travel. Some will pursue a deeper spiritual life.

Remarriage?

One new possibility unique to the Third Day is remarriage. Given the opportunity, many, if not most, widows would like to remarry. If they have been happy in one marriage, there is a good chance they will be happy in another. One study indicated that half to two-thirds of remarriages between elders last until death. That is about the same ratio of success to failure that all American marriages face. Probably the desire of seniors to remarry should be evaluated in about the same way as anyone else's desire to marry: with cautious optimism.

The children of aging parents, however, frequently oppose remarriage. In one study, about 25 percent of remarried older couples said that at one point or another they had almost given in to their children's objections and called off the wedding. After five years of the marriage, more than 80 percent of the children were pleased, and more than half of those who had opposed it had changed their minds.

When the issue of remarriage arises, children (and their parents) worry about two things. First, they think about inheritance. Suppose Dad remarries and then dies within six months. Will his estate go to his new wife, instead of to his children?

Because of this concern, an increasing number of older couples are writing marriage contracts, so that their plans for inheritance are secured before the wedding. In this case, a competent lawyer is necessary.

Some wonder whether a marriage with such a contract is fully Christian, since each partner retains control of his property rather than giving it over to the other. This is a difficult question. Nobody would want, I think, to deny older people the solace of a loving partner. But if this led to "marriages of convenience," in which partners were halfhearted in their commitment to each other, the glory of marriage would be devalued. (So, too, would be the joy of the marriage, which only comes fully with sacrificial love.) No true marriage draws a line down the middle of the household, saying, "On this side is mine and my children's property; on the other side is yours." Accepting a morality of convenience devalues, not only the marriage, but also the people involved—whether young or old.

The ideal solution lies in a contract that honors obligations to both spouse and children, but keeps the marital bond primary. No one owes his children an inheritance. But you do, I think, owe your husband or wife all the care you can offer. If you love someone enough to marry him, that love should surely continue even when you are gone. Marriage contracts should always seek to ensure that the surviving spouse be cared for. If such a stipulation prevents people from marrying, because they want companionship but don't want any possibility of their children losing their inheritance, then perhaps the marriage would not have been one quite worthy of the name.

On the other hand, I can see no objection to a marriage contract that stipulates how inheritances should be handed down once personal needs for both husband and wife are met. So long as both partners agree to such plans, they seem quite honorable.

The second concern children feel cannot be resolved by legal means. It is the concern that, in remarrying, their parent is desecrating the memory of the mother or father who died. This is an objection that widows and widowers themselves may feel. Some will not consider remarriage because of it. As one woman said, "I love once, and that's all."

That, of course, is her business. But is it her children's business? Children often want their parents to stop growing once they have achieved senior status; they prefer to have parents who are living mementos of the past. But for neither children nor parents is this a healthy state of mind. It shows a view of life which follows a bell curve up to a peak in middle age, and then slowly diminishes to nothing in old age. For a Christian, the curve is upward all the way to heaven.

Aging is for growing. Remarriage can be a sign of new life and new possibilities, and children must trust their parents to know what new possibilities they want to entertain. When your entire life has been lived with two parents seemingly fixed from the foundation of the earth, it can be disturbing to consider any change in the combination. Most children don't find the experience as difficult as they anticipate, however. In fact, if their parent is happy, they find it easier to grow closer and enjoy each other.

The woman was sitting on the front porch. It was summer, and the temperature was over 100 degrees. In this neat tract housing in suburbia, nobody sat outside in the middle of such a day. Especially a woman who was obviously well past 65.

Another woman driving by grew curious, and stopped to talk. She learned that the older woman had moved to California from Brooklyn, to stay with her son.

The younger woman brightened. "It must be lovely to live in this quiet place, in your son's beautiful home."

But the older woman was scornful. In a strong Brooklyn accent, she confessed that she wished to heaven she'd never come. "There's nothing here at all!" she said, gesturing toward the street. "Everything's dead. Nobody walks down the sidewalk. Not even kids!"

Moving to a New Home

After a partner dies, many older people decide to change their living quarters. This, too, is a sign of new possibilities, especially in America where "moving on" is part of the pioneer spirit. A new place may be part of a new identity.

Three concerns lead elders to move. First, the old house or apartment is full of memories that can make the "new beginning" more painful than is strictly necessary. Second, widows often wish to be nearer to family members, on whom they rely for supportive friendship. Third, in their new identity they may care less about keeping a large house and garden. They often want (and sometimes need) a dwelling that requires less care, is easier to get around in, and from which they can more easily reach out to others.

Yet these good reasons can lead to very bad decisions. It's extremely important to go slowly. Ultimately, a move may be a good idea, but in the immediate shock of loss, change should be kept to a minimum. According to Jane Otten and Mildred D. Shelley, writing in *When Your Parents Grow Old:* "The most common overreaction cited by professionals dealing with families who have lost a parent is the tendency to move the remaining parent out of his or her home immediately. Come live with us!"

Staying in a familiar, beloved house has many advantages. So does moving to a smaller, convenient, new apartment. Being nearer family is good, but not necessarily better than being in the place where one has roots. There is no "right decision" that fits all people in all situations. A widow whose sense of well-being is rooted in her beautiful house and garden should probably stay put. A widow who tends to grow lonely and unhappy in her large house should probably move. A widow with many old friends in the community should probably stay where she is. A widow who "lives for her grandchildren" might do better to move nearer them. It depends on the person and the circumstances.

The most important thing for relatives and friends to remember is not to make the decision *for* the widow; they should merely help her to make it for herself. Thus, driving her around to look at available apartments or condominiums, for example, and making certain all the appropriate questions are asked is helpful; pressuring her to choose one in particular is not. What seems to you to be merely helpful advice may amount, for an uncertain widow, to coercion.

On the other hand, widows and widowers may be very happy to abdicate responsibility. After years of making decisions with a spouse, they are not used to trusting their own solo judgment. Even an apparently domineering husband has often relied on subtle clues from his wife to judge whether his direction is appropriate. A widow or widower can no longer turn to a partner for help or reassurance— or a veto—in making a move. But it's no favor to the bereaved person to "take over," no matter how willing he or she might be. Sooner or later the surviving spouse must learn to make decisions alone.

Whenever a move is considered, the whole extended family should be fully informed in advance. Siblings can develop long-standing feuds after the death of one of their parents, if decisions are made without adequate consultation. If Daddy suddenly moves across the country into a retirement home near Sister, guess who will be blamed if it turns out unhappily?

Whatever decision is reached, it is always best to use a trial period. Don't sell the old house; rent it out. Don't move into your son's back bedroom for good; try it for three months and see how you like it. Economically this may not make good sense, but so long as going back "home" remains an open possibility, there will be less stress involved in the move. Finding a new identity as a single person takes time, and may require several "trial" lifestyles.

Housing Options

This is a convenient point for considering housing options as they arise for all elders, whether widowed or not. Housing is typically one of the big decisions of the years past 65.

Because retirement communities like "Sun City" in Arizona are highly visible, many people have an idea that older people migrate south in large numbers. Actually all but a small minority stay put. It's true that more seniors move between states than in past generations, but seniors overall remain the least mobile part of the American population. Their roots are deep, and most of them intend to stay where they have long been planted. If they move, it is usually because they want to be nearer to their children and grandchildren. Even then, depression and grief are common over the loss of familiar surroundings and old friends.

Even within the same locale, there are a number of different options:

Retirement communities include any kind of living situation that is specially designed for older people—and for older people only. There is considerable variety in these: "senior adult" mobile home parks, residential subdivisions for seniors only, apartment complexes that offer one or more community meals a day and on-call medical help, and elegant "life care" facilities which provide some or all meals and even nursing home care, if and when needed. Retire-

ment communities run the spectrum from inexpensive
(most mobile home parks) to very expensive (most life care
facilities).

Life care facilities are increasing particularly rapidly.
They offer one considerable advantage over all other options: You will never have to make another move. That is
because they offer every kind of care, including nursing
home care, usually within one complex. Life care facilities
usually require a large initial investment, however, through
which you "buy in." Careful research should be done before
choosing this option.

Retirement communities are usually quiet and secure,
and they may offer services that are difficult to obtain elsewhere, such as community meals. The main attraction of
retirement communities, though, is sociability. People your
own age, with similar interests, are nearby.

Many people, however, dislike the idea of "age-segregated" housing. One senior told me vehemently, "It's not
natural for older people to be shoved in just with older
people." He lives in an attractive "seniors only" mobile
home park, and feels it would be economically impossible
to move, but he wishes that he had never gone there in
the first place.

Does his objection really hold up? The same man told
me with obvious relish of the "hot pool games" he and
other retired men have in their community center. He was
obviously gaining benefits from being near a number of older
men, whatever benefits he might also be forfeiting.

At any age, it's good to know people from other generations. But your neighborhood isn't the only place to meet
them. Just as often, the generations meet through church,
through volunteer activities, and particularly through family. People living in retirement centers may have as much

meaningful contact with younger people and children as do those who live in ordinary communities.

What retirement centers distinctly offer are peer friend-ships. When older people grow less mobile, ties with friends who live at a distance tend to suffer. There is considerable sociological evidence that age-segregated housing, because of the friendships it encourages, can lead to dramatic im-provement in morale. Not everyone will want to live in such facilities, but I think people should try to be open-minded—especially if they have always said, "I'll never live in a place like that."

Shared housing. Surveys suggest that older people do best when they are not alone. Sometimes a number of older people sharing a house or apartment semi-communally is a healthy choice. At the moment, we have very limited ex-perience with this kind of option; not many older people have been anxious to experiment. But under the right cir-cumstances and with the right people, it can be an attractive option.

Separate dwelling, near to relatives. Traditionally, in parts of Europe, parents retire to a small house separate from, but near to their children's house. Thus they are private, but able to be closely linked to daily family life. They call it, "intimacy at a distance." Many families opt for this today. Some of the qualities to look for in a home are:

> privacy
> safety
> easy maintenance
> porch and/or garden shaded part of the day
> living room large enough to entertain grandchildren
> easy laundry facilities
> storage room for prized possessions
> easy access to bathtub or shower

To be avoided:

> slippery floors
> low fences or walls
> cabinets that jut out
> winding paths
> steep stairs

Living with children. From lack of economic choice, or because of a sense of family togetherness, elders may "move in" with children. This used to be a very common practice, especially among widows; it has grown steadily less so in the last decades.

You can hear very strong opinions on this option. For some, its prevalence is a handy measure of the strength of extended families, indeed of the morality of society. If Japanese elders live with their children more than Americans do, that is supposedly an indication of how low American morals have slipped. Yet one survey showed that those who favor intergenerational living tend to be those who have never experienced it; this explains why younger people tend to feel more positive than their elders. People who oppose it are often those who have seen it up close.

Anyone wanting to try this kind of living arrangement should know in advance that it can be very trying for all concerned. Even those who are grateful for the experience testify that it is rarely easy. Some of the issues that prove difficult are:

• Lack of privacy. Living together is almost always easier in a large house, preferably one in which elders can have private space and a bathroom of their own. Failing that, it helps to specify certain rooms and times which are strictly reserved for rest and quiet activities.

- Intergenerational conflict. Those differences with Mom or Dad which you thought you left behind fifty years ago may be, surprisingly, still potent. Just as troubling can be conflicts between grandparents and grandchildren. Noise, changed standards of dress and behavior, rivalries (Grandma and one favored grandchild against the rest of the family) are typical difficulties.
- Money. Often, children and their aging parents don't talk about how to share living expenses. Yet those who choose to share a house usually have limited funds. Resentments and suspicions can simmer from both sides. It is important to talk about money in advance. No matter how difficult the discussion is, make sure that every issue is covered thoroughly.
- The strain of care. Older parents may be in good shape when they move in, but they probably won't stay that way indefinitely. Often, the burden of care grows, sometimes to the point where it becomes simply impossible to bear. The idea of one generation caring for another is attractive, but if the younger generation is physically worn down and has no patience or strength left for personal warmth, the effort is probably misguided.

There are many families who have tried sharing a house between generations, and would not trade the experience for anything. Whether such intimacy is a good thing or not depends heavily on the personalities involved, and the level of care required for the elders and any other family members. This option, like all housing options, should be entered with eyes wide open.

All in all, the choice of where and how to live is extremely personal. Jane Boyajian writes of standing happily with her father in the light, airy space of a new condominium she had chosen for him; she was particularly pleased that the building was "placed in a park-like setting well back from the street and abundant with the giant shade trees of New England." Then, to her astonishment, her father turned to her and said, "What is difficult for me is that we are so far from the street; I cannot see what is passing by."

Few people, at any age, would trust another person to choose a house for them. When deciding on a move after the death of a spouse, or at any other time past retirement, the people involved must take great care to respect the idiosyncracies of the people who will have to live in the new place.

DAY 4

MEMO TO MY FATHER-IN-LAW:

WE HEARD THIS MORNING THAT YOU TOOK A fall, sprawling headlong onto the bedroom floor in the middle of the night. Which brought to mind the awful spill you took when you were visiting a few months ago, missing that small step on our patio and toppling straight over, like a six-foot statue. Fortunately, you were only bruised. And last night nothing was really damaged. But how many falls do you get before something breaks? Your balance isn't what it used to be.

Besides that, you've been sick. A flu knocks you out like it never used to. You talked as though we'd better cancel plans to meet in San Diego this summer. Of course, all that can change, but it struck me hard that someday, not too far into the future, you'll be unable to take that long flight west. And not coincidentally, you're going to need us then—need our help, but mostly our support and love. That will not be easy to give, from 2,000 miles away. I can't see any way we'll be able to give all that we, or you, wish.

The question may be: How do we live happily in a relationship where we want to do so much more than we can?

The Fourth Day: Role Reversal

❧ R OY PRUITT RETIRED EARLY FROM A CAREER IN management. With his wife Arlene he moved to Mendocino, a picturesque village on the wild northern California coast. There they built a house near Roy's parents, who had moved to Mendocino after a lifetime of working in the L.A. County Library. Roy's dad loved to fish, and the rural character of the area appealed to both families.

For about five years the situation was ideal. Then Roy's dad became quite ill with asthma. Gradually he lost his mobility.

"I didn't realize how much Dad was aging," Roy says. "We went salmon fishing every year. One year I had to almost lift him into the boat. Suddenly you realize that some increment of aging has taken place."

The younger Pruitts sold their home and leased a place closer to their parents. Then, within a year, "We got to the place where Mother couldn't take care of Dad. He would fall and be unable to get up." The cost of 24-hour nursing care seemed prohibitive. Instead, the younger Pruitts moved in with their parents, hired a young woman to provide care six days a week, and bought a second-hand mobile home about a mile from the house as a daytime retreat and a place to entertain friends. In the late afternoon Arlene would leave the trailer and go home to fix dinner.

"It's impossible to explain to someone who hasn't gone through it what it's like to take care of elderly people," Roy says. "It's a difficult thing. All your life your parents have been the authority. All of a sudden there comes a time when you are telling them what to do!"

Roy's mother, a neat, tidy person, had advanced osteoporosis, and was barely mobile herself. She did not adjust well to her husband's deterioration. "Dad got sloppy," Roy explains. "He would cough all over the table, spill things." This was unacceptable to Mother; it distressed her so that eventually she took her dinner in her own room.

"Dad never got to the place of having to get up during the night. That was a godsend. Most of the time we got a night's sleep. He was in a wheelchair for about a year. One night he asked for corned beef and cabbage for dinner, and within an hour had a massive heart attack."

Roy's mother was in her own room, where she'd finished dinner. Roy and Arlene wanted to shield her from what was occurring, but when Roy's dad began to have convulsions, they thought they ought to tell her. She didn't go to him, but sat up by her bedside, waiting. Within a few minutes, her husband was gone. She seemed to be in shock when they told her the news.

She lived another five years. For a time after her husband's death, she seemed happier. Her greatest source of stress and worry had been removed. But she too went through a gradual physical deterioration. "She had little accidents. We had to install indoor and outdoor carpet. We both got very tired of turning her in bed. She was quite heavy."

Roy and Arlene took separate bedrooms, so that Roy could wake up when he heard his mother move in her hospital bed. He would get up six times a night and help her reach a bedside commode. Unfortunately, embarrassment inhibited her ability to urinate. Finally, they put her in incontinent pants.

"She looked out at the ocean all day, and did jigsaw puzzles," Roy continues. "More and more she needed help to do them. At first I helped her get the border pieces. Then that wasn't enough. I would get a row of pieces set and put them into a box, so she could put them in one at a time. Eventually we got puzzles with large pieces.

"But we were getting so tired, not just physically but psychologically. It started getting to Arlene. Every so often I would lose my patience with my mother, and then I would feel so bad about scolding her. I would have to hold her when she brushed her teeth, help her off the john.

"She just wasn't the same person. You almost feel that you're taking care of a stranger. That's one reason I wouldn't want to have my daughter Julie taking care of me."

After a long, exhausting struggle the Pruitts began to realize they could cope no longer. "We would go in and talk with my mother and say, 'Someday I'm not going to be able to take care of you.' She would just smile. She didn't want to think about it."

"The day we moved her to the convalescent home was worse than the day she died," Arlene says. "Mother was kind of stonefaced. That made it all the harder. She couldn't believe it, though we had talked with her. We went every day to see her. She didn't complain. But she didn't make friends. She didn't eat much. She made up her mind that she didn't want to get used to it. I think she made up her mind that she was going to die." And she did—three months later.

It took several months for the Pruitts to recover. "I wouldn't have wanted to talk with you then," Roy told me. "We were just so tired." The decision to put her in the convalescent home haunted them. "It's hard to second-guess, but I'm convinced she would have lived longer at home. I just felt like a beast after that," Arlene says. "That's one big advantage of going into a retirement home. You don't put your children through that decision of whether to move you into a nursing home."

Years have softened the edge of grief, and the Pruitts no longer question what they did. "We don't think about the difficult times, we remember it fondly. We think about Mother and Dad and the things they did." Nonetheless, they are resolute that they will not live with their daughter if and when such a time comes. They have made plans to enter a life care facility in Oregon.

Beginning to Need Some Help

Up to this chapter, while considering the first three Days of old age, we have examined losses that can be overcome. A person can "get over" even the terrible pain of losing a spouse, and return to an undiminished vitality.

Such losses are all that a great many elderly people—perhaps even the majority—ever experience. Many never experience the kind of general, degenerative losses that the Pruitts describe. For many, losses are minor—a gradual slowing down before death. But as more people live longer, losses like the Pruitts experienced become more common.

Some idea of this can be gained by looking at the percentage of people in different age groups who need "functional assistance," that is, help with chores like bathing, dressing, eating and getting in and out of bed.

Ages 18 to 44	1%
45–64	3%
65–74	7%
75–84	16%
85 +	39%

These numbers are encouraging, I think. Even a person who lives into his late eighties has a better than even chance of never needing basic assistance. Nonetheless, the longer a person lives, the greater are his chances of needing such help.

Such statistics can give a mistaken sense that aging moves predictably, however, researchers have found great individual differences in the rate at which people change. An 80-year-old woman may be, physiologically, as "young" as a 60-year-old. And a 60-year-old may be as "old" as an 80-year-old. You can predict fairly accurately that every child will learn how to walk in the one-year span between eight months and 20 months. But you cannot predict when, if ever, that same person will lose the ability to walk.

Keeping individual differences in mind, aging does bring a gradual diminishing of physical vitality. It is part of growing. No one can totally escape it. The 40-year-old cannot react as quickly as he could at 20, though he may not need to, having given up activities that demand quick reactions. Also, experience and sagacity give him skills that can compensate for his losses, in most circumstances. At some point—roughly at age 70—the older person begins to feel that physical limitations are genuinely limiting.

Here is a brief list of physical losses that come, almost inevitably, though to different degrees, with age:

• Loss of taste (often leading to a poor appetite, or a "junk food" appetite, which can cause malnutrition—even in someone gaining weight).
• Loss of smell (leading, among other things, to the inability to detect leaking gas).
• Loss of muscular strength.
• Loss of vision (affecting the enjoyment of books and TV, as well as the ability to drive). The ability to distinguish colors also diminishes.
• Loss of hearing. (About 50 percent of males and 35 percent of females over 65 have enough hearing loss to affect interaction with others.) High tones particularly are lost, so that when speakers "raise their voices," the hearer often hears less rather than more. The enjoyment of music may diminish or disappear altogether.
• Slowing of reaction time (affecting driving, and leading to falls).
• Decreased sense of balance and increased dizziness.
• Reduced sexual response.
• Less effective kidneys (leading to altered responses to alcohol and other drugs, including medical drugs).
• Less elastic bladder (leading, along with other causes, to more frequent urination).
• Less effective lungs and heart, the heart pumping perhaps 30 percent less blood than in a 30-year-old, the lungs less than half as effective as a young person's (leading to quick fatigue).
• Diminished digestion (leading to constipation).
• Loss of skin elasticity (leading to wrinkles).
• Stiffer joints (leading to slow movement and a shuffling gait).
• Smaller abdomen and thickened waist, though weight may be down. (Clothes rarely fit well.)

Almost every purely physical measurement shows decreased vitality with age. The overall picture is well conveyed by the statement, "I just can't do what I used to do."

Slowing Down or Getting Sick?

None of these losses means that an older person is sick or helpless. In mild doses, at least, all these losses can be compensated for. And they are. Older drivers tend to become more careful, for instance, and may have fewer accidents than younger drivers, even though their reactions are slower.

Making compensations, however, puts stress on an older person. People under stress, at any age, are brittle—more likely to become angry or depressed or to act irrationally. And when a health crisis comes—a fall, a bout with influenza, a car accident—its effects are likely to be far more devastating to an older person than to a younger one.

One gerontologist has put this rather graphically in comparing two cavemen, old Urk and young Murk. So long as life proceeds benignly, Urk's age may make very little difference, even though he has "slowed down." In fact, his greater experience may give him an advantage over Murk in gathering nutritious plants. But suppose a saber-toothed tiger attacks. Then, under drastic stress, Urk's slower responses will make a dramatic difference in survival. Under conditions without stress, older people may function as well or better than younger people. In a crisis, they don't. Nobody dies of old age, but old age makes a person more vulnerable to forces that can kill or cripple.

There is one bright spot in this portrait of vulnerability: A person's mental abilities do not, fortunately, decline. The body may crumble, but the mind usually does not. Older people tend to lose some short-term memory, but they can make allowances for this with more careful routines and habits—always checking the stove when they leave the kitchen, for instance. Overall, intelligence holds its own throughout life, and it may even increase, particularly for those who keep their minds stimulated.

Since so many of the elderly worry about losing their minds, this is very good news indeed. A small proportion of seniors, particularly those who live into their eighties or nineties, will develop Alzheimer's or other conditions that lead to senile dementia. But these problems are utterly different from "forgetting your keys." Forgetfulness is a minor annoyance, usually completely unrelated to any major health problem.

One factor does block learning for older people—anxiety about appearing foolish or making mistakes. Studies show that when seniors are in a comfortable and secure environment, they tend to perform far better than when they feel exposed to failure. Seniors need encouragement to use their undiminished intelligence to cope with the tremendous changes of the Fourth Day. If they feel confident and secure, they will be more likely to succeed.

How Elders Respond to Their Losses

Physical losses are only the beginning. They trigger other changes as elders compensate (sometimes inappropriately) for what they have lost or fear losing. Their behavior may seem bizarre, unless the connection is made to the physical loss.

If short-term memory declines, then the older person may compensate by developing "neurotic" routines and habits. If digestion is poor, the older person may respond by becoming very careful about eating. If the older person can't hear what others are saying, he may dominate conversations. It is not hard to understand why some older people grow nervous about going out, if they cannot catch themselves when they lose their balance. It is not hard to understand why some older people withdraw from social contact, if they are embarrassed by their inability to eat without drooling, or to sit through a meeting without having to go to the bathroom.

To a younger person, elders may seem to have grown intolerably fussy or anxious. From an older person's perspective, "fussiness" has a purpose, even if she can't articulate it. It would be nice if she could simply explain how she is feeling. Often, though, younger people will have to use *their* undiminished intelligence to figure out what is going on.

Not surprisingly, many older people experience depression. Each loss is like a little death. Grief is a natural response. "Because the deaths do not come with dramatic impact, but overlap one another," writes Arthur Becker, "the neat schedules of the grief process outlined by people like Kubler-Ross and others are not always relevant. One can be at the acceptance stage in grieving over lost youthful energy and at the denial stage of grieving over inability to manage one's fingers as dexterously over the handwork, the piano, the typewriter, or the musical instrument."

Physical losses can strip away independence and dignity as help is needed for tasks that older people used to do for themselves. Some personal preferences inevitably get lost, particularly if older people must depend on institutions. The Meals on Wheels program pays attention to nutrition but may not know that someone likes a slice of lemon in her water glass. In our society, some depersonalization usually accompanies any degree of dependency.

An older person may compensate for this loss of independence by becoming very outspoken and opinionated; he may develop very particular ways of eating a meal or keeping house, as a way of establishing individuality. My sister noted, when she worked in the dining room of a nursing home, that almost every person had an idiosyncratic way he expected to be served. One woman, for instance, always wanted her coffee cup half filled—not more—when she began her meal, though she would not take a single sip until she had completed her meal. She was compensating for the impersonality of eating in a cafeteria. Whenever an older person acts "difficult" it is a good idea to ask why. Making a moral issue out of "difficult behavior" will rarely help. Sympathetic understanding is the surest way of working your way through it.

Lesley, a divorcée, works full time, as she has throughout her adult life. Her job is low-paying, and she and her 80-year-old mother, Amy, must live on a tight budget. Amy moved in two years before the divorce, having unexpectedly sold her house and pulled up roots in the South.

In the last few years Amy's health, independence, and mental outlook have declined. She has been in and out of the hospital—once for a broken collar bone and pelvis, once to install a pacemaker, once for gall bladder surgery. She has had hepatitis and a small stroke. Fortunately, all medical expenses were paid by Medicaid. She is a large woman and has a hard time getting around now. Her eyesight is failing and, with it, her interest in reading and letter writing.

As a younger woman Amy was unfailingly upbeat, but now she stays in her housecoat all day, often drifting into a monologue about the past. Sometimes she has fits of crying which Lesley has to talk her through. Ironically, Amy was an only child who cared for her parents in their old age, and she used to say she would never be that kind of burden to her children. But she has forgotten all about that now, and has ways of making Lesley feel guilty for any perceived neglect. Whenever Lesley goes out for any purpose other than work, for example, Amy complains.

Lesley's daughter Susan lives nearby, and would gladly

help out so that Lesley could have time for herself, but she rarely takes advantage of the standing offer. She has always had a difficult time accepting help.

Lesley is completely drained, and her children are worried about her health. With their encouragement, Lesley has decided that if Amy has to enter a hospital again, she will take her mother to a nursing home rather than bring her home. The problem is that since Lesley must continue to work as well as to care for her mother, the burden is growing intolerable.

Role Reversal Between Parents and Children

During the first three Days of aging, children and other relatives are rarely on center stage. True, children may provide care and comfort during critical losses, and they may become closer friends with their parents. But they are not responsible, in any direct, ongoing way, for the care of their parents. Nor should they try to be.

But in this Fourth Day children may be called upon to assume a critical role. They become the caregivers, gradually taking responsibility for their parents' welfare. In the Fourth Day parents need help to get along—perhaps only a little, but it must be consistent.

People tell stories about parents abandoned by their children, as though it were the most common thing in the world. Studies belie this. In one survey of older people, 66 percent had seen a child the very day they were interviewed, and only 2 percent had not seen a child within the last year. Some "abandoned" parents are those who actually abandoned their children years before. Some children do neglect their parents. But the vast majority continue to honor their parents, sometimes at great personal cost.

The children often anticipate tremendous expenses, and

wonder whether they will have enough money. It turns out, however, that financial costs are rarely the major issue. Less than 1 percent of elderly Americans receive their principal financial support from their children or other relatives, and less than 5 percent receive support regularly enough that it could be considered income. As a matter of fact, the latest figures indicate that far fewer elders live below the poverty line than do their children. Elders are more than twice as likely to be providing financial help than to be receiving it.

The "cost" to children is more often physical and emotional—and it can be very great. Some role reversal begins to occur. The mother becomes the daughter, and the daughter the mother. This switch is extremely uncomfortable for both. It usually begins so gradually that neither mother nor daughter really grasp what is happening. Eventually, it becomes the dominant pattern in their relationship. Lesley frets about Amy's diet in much the same way that Amy once fretted about her daughter's. And Amy seeks Lesley's attention as a child might—by complaining and making herself miserable.

Elders are losing control of their lives, and they feel powerless to stop the process. Indeed, very often they fear that their children and others will, while meaning well, seize control. The children will decide when Grandma can no longer live in her house, must move to another state, should enter a nursing home, ought to get rid of that dog. What can a dependent elder do? She relies on these caregivers; she cannot tell them to get lost. Trapped by her need for care, she is returning to that state of powerlessness her subconscious remembers so well: a small child looking up at the big people who rule her life because she cannot function without their help.

The Persistent Problem of Guilt

The children's position is no more comfortable. The inner self recoils, horrified, at helping Mother go to the bathroom, at spooning soft food into Dad's mouth, at warning Mom for the tenth time that she will not be able to live on her own if she can't learn to turn off the oven. People feel guilty for treating their parents this way, and the guilt feelings are often expressed in anger toward their parents or toward themselves. The only child who can live up to his own expectations of how to treat his parents in the Fourth Day is a child with a very poor sense of responsibility toward his parents. All others will feel guilty. Guilt plagues the children of parents in the Fourth Day, and especially those children who are in the role of caregiver. No previous experience in life has taught them that they will be unable to satisfy their parents—or themselves—in such basic matters. The guilt feelings aren't unrelieved—there is grace and laughter too—but virtually all caregivers struggle with feeling guilty.

While parents and children are working their separate ways through these Freudian thickets, their relationship can deteriorate. For parents, it is difficult to be consistently cheerful and grateful for care they wish desperately they did not need. Many elders openly complain about how their children care for them, and try to get others to take their side against the very people who are knocking themselves out on their behalf. Naturally, this is a bitter song for the children to hear—especially if they already feel guilty.

Even without such complaining, it is difficult for children to be consistently cheerful and unpretentious about giving care they also wish desperately were unnecessary. Becker comments: "Often I have found that when middle-aged children must parent their own parents, one of the things they attempt to do is to outshine their original parents. They are determined to do a better job of parenting than their own parents did. This generates natural feelings of guilt and resentment on both sides of the relationship." Often the caregiving child will treat her parents with the same concerns that her parents taught her. If the mother was constantly harping on what her daughter ate, the daughter may worry her mother sick over the same issue.

Sometimes parents and children grow so enmeshed in their relationship that they lose any sense of their own separate identities. The caregiving child gives up any outside life, living and breathing by the moods of her parent. There is no space between them. This kind of identity merging is particularly tempting for those who are exhausted—and both parents and their caregiving children often are.

What helps parents and children through this reversal of roles? They will usually build on the kind of relationship they have already established, good or bad. That is one reason why it is so critical to foster good communication earlier in retirement. Under the growing stresses of the Fourth Day, few people will have enough energy left to make breakthroughs in their relationship. They will often (though not always) perpetuate the patterns already begun.

Yet sometimes an outside observer can facilitate a new approach. Social workers or pastors, particularly those who have considerable experience with the elderly and their families, may be able to offer some objective advice, help parent and child to understand the other's point of view, and work up a new plan of operation. Certainly Lesley could have used that help long before her relationship with Amy deteriorated to its present state. There may still be time.

Barbara's husband died when he was 49. As a widow with five children, she decided to move back near her parents.

"If I had known that my father was going to die, that might have colored my decision," Barbara says. When the news of his death came, however, she was already packed, and felt it was too late to change her plans. Anyway, her mother needed her. But she and her mother had never had an easy relationship.

Barbara says that when Laura, her mother, was good company, she was among the very best; when she was bad, she was horrid. Barbara grew up feeling she could never live up to her mother's standards. Her greatest fear was that her mother would apply pressure to move in with her. Barbara made it clear that her children took priority, but she feared that in a few more years, when the last one left the nest, her mother would increase her demands.

Laura lived alone, in a mobile home. She had tried a retirement center, but left after six months, finding it too confining. She took frequent bus trips, and had an active social life playing bridge. Laura was something of a hypochondriac. Nonetheless, she had some legitimate health concerns and had experienced a hysterectomy, surgery for gallstones, and a mastectomy. In addition, she was told that she suffered from emphysema and congestive heart failure.

Still, Barbara found it extremely difficult to know when to take her mother's complaints seriously. She felt that Laura wanted constant attention, and this kind of smothering was just the thing Barbara hated. Laura's feelings were easily hurt, and she often cried until her feathers were smoothed. Even the nicest things Barbara planned seemed to turn out wrong. She took her mother for a weekend birthday trip. On the second day, Laura announced that she needed to go home to do some shopping, so they cut the trip short, leaving Barbara bewildered and frustrated.

Barbara tried to be supportive of her mother. She called every night at 7:30, which seemed to give Laura great security. Barbara says that despite the problems,

she and Laura managed to have the best relationship
possible. Barbara tried to emphasize that it's all right to
make mistakes. "It's over," Barbara would say after a
disagreement. "Let's go on from here." (Her mother was
a tenacious fighter.) Nonetheless, Barbara was sure she
would never really satisfy her mother.

Last year, when Barbara came home from a week's
vacation, Laura announced that her doctor had said her
heart was failing. With her children now gone, Barbara
felt she had no choice. She told Laura that the time had
come for her to move in. Laura was elated.

Later, when Barbara talked to the doctor, he said
he couldn't remember saying any such thing to Laura.
Laura had an aneurism, but he didn't think it was life-
threatening. Barbara felt that her mother had once again
manipulated her.

In any case, as Barbara now says; "I do believe it was
God's timing." Six weeks after Laura moved in, she was
admitted to the hospital. On the second day her lungs
failed and she was gone. "Isn't God kind?" Barbara says.
"We had six good weeks and then the end was as easy
for us as possible."

What Children Can Do

A great many people feel cheated when their parents
grow old, simply because their dream of developing peaceful, appreciative relationships doesn't come true. The practical difficulties and changes often seem to make their
relationship worse. Children who are giving their very lives
to help their parents may find themselves paradoxically
more frustrated with those parents than ever before. Grandmother becomes not so much a human being struggling
through adversity as a difficult project.

The elderly are very conscious of this nightmare. Though
they repeatedly say, "We don't want to be a burden to our
children," this rarely means that they want to live com-

pletely independently. Most are intensely aware of their desire to experience intimacy with their children. They do not want to be a project, or a burden; they want to be a joy. They don't want their children to have to take care of them; they do want their children to *care for* them. There is a difference which children sometimes fail to grasp.

Ronald Blythe writes: "The young do not see the old struggling along in day-to-day births and night-to-night deaths, and organizing themselves to cope alternatively with the light and dark hours. However fragile they are, they regard them as monoliths, hard and enduring from all that has happened to them."

If children learn anything from caring for their aging parents, it ought to be that their parents are not monoliths, but creatures like themselves, increasingly vulnerable. A good rule of thumb for their care is: "Do unto others as you would have them do unto you." For it often happens that well-meaning children treat their parents in a way that they themselves would resent.

The first principle is respect. Many children must "parent" their own aging parents, but this does not mean that their parents become children again. They are adults, now entering a new phase of life which their children have never experienced. Parents do not need to be scolded or patronized. They may need (as most adults do) some clear words about how they should act; and for the children, saying these words may feel very much like parenting small children. But the more the children can maintain a sense of adult-to-adult respect for their parents, the less threatened the parents are likely to feel by their loss of authority.

"Mother, if you don't eat your carrots, I'm going to stop cooking for you!" is the voice of an adult speaking to an irresponsible child. An adult speaking to an adult would say something like, "Mother, why won't you eat your carrots? You need those vitamins." Or, "Mother, if I'm going to cook a balanced meal, you're going to have to do your part and *eat* a balanced meal."

The second principle is, concentrate on helping elders maintain a role in society. It's easy to focus on maintenance tasks—cleaning, cooking—and miss elders' greater needs. They spend more and more time in a few rooms; they can do less and less for themselves, let alone for others. Keeping in contact with the world is increasingly difficult, and there is less energy for it. Professor Albert Outler spoke to Eugene Bianchi about this: "I find that, given my normal energies, I turn very much more apathetic unless there is somebody there, somebody asking me to do something. Given another person's presence at home, your coming, or having to speak to a class or something or another, arouses vitality that isn't there naturally. . . . Often I feel like, 'Gee, I can't pull it off this time.' Then from somewhere the resources come, vitality surges up, and I get on through. Then I collapse again. That is what getting old has meant for me so far."

So children, rather than doing everything for their parents, should ask their parents to do something for someone else. Of course, what elders are able to do may be limited. The elder's role in society usually becomes gradually less focused on projects, and more on relationships. Their role—their sense of being necessary—may eventually come down to a family who enjoys their presence. Here, too, they should be asked to help. "I want my children to grow up knowing their grandfather."

The third, corollary principle is, don't do too much for elders. Everything you do for them is something they are not challenged to do for themselves. A keen sense of appropriateness is needed. If people expect too much of their elders, the stress overwhelms them and they may withdraw or grow ill. Yet probably more often, children take over inappropriately. Bumagin and Hirn refer to an elderly person making a heroic effort to get to a polling place to vote. They ask, "Why is it that when an old person thumbs his nose at fate and succeeds, one's first reaction is apt to be, 'Oh, but you shouldn't have!' instead of 'Bravo!'"

Their question is not hard to answer. We react that way because we want to protect our elders. From what? Might we not, very often, want to protect them from *old age itself*? If so, we can only fail. It is as impossible as protecting children from rejection, or football players from bruises. Older people must face, must struggle with, their losses. Their dignity lies in struggling well, not in avoiding the struggle.

A fourth principle: Let elders make their own decisions, as long as they are capable of doing so without trampling on the rights of others. Becker writes: "Almost every family with a frail elderly member struggles with the difficult matter of 'How long shall Grandma (or Grandpa) be permitted to live all alone?' The principle to be followed is clear, even though the execution of it may be difficult for a loving family to accept: as long as she (or he) is able to enter rationally and intelligently into the decision, as long as she takes into account the whole network of her relationships and those related to her, it is her decision. I am sure that if our elders felt that we as their children, well-meaning friends, and pastors were committed to this principle, they would much more willingly enter into dialog with us about what decision to make. It is their fear that we are going to take over their lives and make their decisions for them that makes them reluctant, just as teenagers are, to take us into their confidence as they reflect on what to decide."

What Bothers the Caregivers

That is, in a nutshell, what elders need most in the Fourth Day. What do their children need? The role of caregiver may be as emotionally difficult as that of the person receiving the care. One study found that caregivers are three times more likely than the elder they care for to report feeling depressed, and four times more likely to report feeling angry. The overriding emotion for caregivers is guilt, frequently accompanied by exhaustion. Fairly often people compound their guilt and exhaustion with dread. They can't stop wondering how they will manage whatever comes next.

Four questions plague caregivers—questions for which there are no real answers. First, *How much should I sacrifice?* Am I being abused by other family members who do less? Am I cheating my own family? How much should I ask my own spouse and children to give up so that I can provide this care? Where do I draw the line? And if I do draw the line, what will happen to my aging parent?

Second, *How much do I take over?* Those who work closely with the elderly emphasize the importance of allowing as much independence as possible. However, this judgment call is often difficult to make. How much independence is enough? Too much? The caregiver is torn by competing desires: to do everything for the elder, or to run away and do nothing! In a matter of days, even hours, the situation can change dramatically. Last week it may have been quite correct to let Father cook for himself; but this week, since he has a cold, he needs nutritious meals. And next week? You'll find you are always doing too much or too little, or both.

Third, *How much can I say?* Hardly any caregiver is completely pleased with her parents' behavior. Patterns of manipulation, of verbal abuse, of complaining abound. Lesley and Amy are sadly typical. Lesley is exhausted because, among other things, Amy drenches herself in self-pity. Does Lesley want to tell Amy a thing or two? Of course she does. Would it make things better or worse if she did? That is very difficult to say. Unfortunately, it is a very rare child who has achieved perfect communication with her parents.

Fourth, *Am I doing any good?* The caregiver sacrifices a great deal. Her job may be the equivalent of full-time work, yet very rarely can she drop other responsibilities with her own family, church, or work, and even more rarely is she allowed time off—weekends, vacations, evenings. It is exhausting work. The nagging question remains: How much am I accomplishing? We are accustomed to seeing positive results from hard work. By the nature of the situation, that is not the case with parents in the Fourth Day. Their situation rarely improves for long. No matter how hard the caregiver works, health declines with age. So she feels this nagging, unsettling question: Am I doing any good? Is it all pointless?

Needs of the Caregivers

One child will almost always turn out to be the principal caregiver. Somehow, plans to share the work equally rarely quite succeed; one person ends up in charge. This principal caregiver is typically either a daughter or a daughter-in-law, so much so that some claim that the term "caregiver" is a euphemism for "unpaid female relative." One survey found that the average person gives 16 hours a week to the care of an elderly parent. More than one in four caregivers hasn't had a break for over a year. Sadly, she may be criticized by her siblings, particularly those who are not involved in the care.

What does this one caregiver need? First, she needs respite—at least a few hours a week which are fully her own, when other family members or community institutions take responsibility from her shoulders. Vacations are also essential, and are unlikely to occur unless other family members take over. (Nursing homes can be used profitably for short periods, so the caregiver can get away; but still, others need to visit the nursing home and show concern.) The caregiver, because of her sense of responsibility, may resist the help. But if she does not get it, she will probably eventually get sick herself or reach the point where she is emotionally unable to provide care any longer.

Second, she needs others to share the load. She will probably continue to take chief responsibility, but there are certain tasks that others can do, such as taxes, or shopping, or laundry. The fact that others are willing to help, that she is not completely alone in her responsibilities, is a psychological encouragement as well as a physical aid.

Third, she needs information about what services are available for the elderly in the community. It takes time to track this information down, digest it, and think out what is really helpful. Someone else can help by doing some of the legwork, starting at the Area Agency on Aging (they go by various names, but most communities have them), where a staff member should be able to offer an overview of services available.

Fourth, she needs information to help her understand aging and the care the elderly require. Knowing what is normal removes a great deal of anxiety, fear, and shame from the experience. Seminars are sometimes offered, and there is a wealth of literature. Finding that literature, screening it, even providing a few hours of respite so she can read it, can be extremely helpful. Caregivers may need training in basic nursing and caregiving skills. Men, in particular, feel the need for such instruction. Some of them have never washed clothes or bathed someone.

Fifth, the caregiver needs recognition. Commonly she feels that no one realizes how much she does. No one even wants to talk about it. If anything, other family members and friends seem to resent how much less of her time they receive. The caregiver may be involved in the hardest life-and-death struggle of her life, but as far as others are concerned, it is routine. She needs constant, warm recognition for her work.

> Marion's mother, Ruby, is in her eighties. The two had a good relationship while Marion was growing up. Ruby taught piano and lived a quiet, secure life.
>
> The first time Marion saw her mother have an "anger attack" was after Marion's marriage to Leon. Riding in the car one day, Ruby became very upset and abusive over Marion and Leon's choice of church. An astonishing tirade broke out. Leon and Marion didn't know how to respond.
>
> The outburst was not repeated until years later when Ruby came to live near Marion. Ruby's sight had deteriorated; she was now legally blind and could no longer teach piano. She wrote Marion and Leon, asking them to find a house for her in their town. They rented one they thought very nice, and when Ruby arrived, the whole family—including the children—proudly accompanied her to see it.
>
> Ruby came unglued when she saw the house. She hated it and accused Marion and Leon of conspiring against her. When Ruby went out and rented her own house, the family was stunned by her behavior.
>
> Since then, the incidents Marion and Leon have come to call "anger attacks" have become more frequent. At a family gathering, everything will seem fine. Then in the middle of the night Ruby will call Marion, absolutely

furious over something that happened at the gathering. When she gets going, there's no reasoning with her. The next day, she can't remember being angry.

Once, when Marion's son-in-law was driving by Ruby's house, he saw police cars. He stopped and found that a gun Ruby owned had gone off in her hand and shot a hole through the floor. Ruby had called the police to come and get the gun. When the family arrived, she accused them of fiddling with the gun so it would go off. She said that, unless they had given the key to someone else, they were the only other ones to enter her house. Ruby demanded that they return her extra key. Now, Ruby has no recollection of the incident, and has asked Marion several times to take the extra key. Marion prefers not to.

On another occasion, while visiting her son, Ruby became very interested in putting her house in her children's names to make probate easier when she died. Her son introduced her to his lawyer, who arranged the transfer. At the time Ruby was very pleased with herself. Later on, however, she became upset. She began to talk about the crooked attorney and vacillated about her decision for weeks. After awhile, her son was sorry he had offered to help.

Incidents like these have made the whole family ambivalent about caring for Ruby's needs. They wonder whether there is some physiological origin to her outbursts. The family doctor doesn't know what to think. He referred them to a neurologist in a nearby city, but when they got there the doctor was out of town, and a replacement doctor spent two exhausting hours asking questions. In the end, he offered no explanation or suggestions. Marion wishes they had a local physician who could be more helpful.

Ruby has always been very independent, and has trouble letting Marion do anything for her. She sold her car fifteen years ago, but never asked for rides, choosing to take a taxi or ride the bus. Nowadays she seldom goes out, except to walk around the block with her bird, or to cross the street to a small store. She watches TV a lot, and Marion and Leon take her grocery shopping once a week. They used to bring her large-print books, but she'd get so stirred up over something she'd read that Marion and Leon stopped bringing them.

Marion talks to her every day, and Ruby will sometimes call nine or ten times in a day. Every once in a while Ruby will say, "I just can't stay here any more, I've got to move to L.A. I'm going to sell this house. Nobody takes care of me."

At her repeated request Marion and Leon took Ruby to see a retirement center, but when they got there, Ruby asked, "What are we doing here?" and wanted no part of it. For a while Marion looked for a residential care home where Ruby could have her own room, but had to give up on the idea. "My mother can't be convinced of anything," Marion says. "She continually changes her mind." Now she has resigned herself to waiting until something happens to her mother—a fall, for instance.

Marion confesses that she is always dealing with guilt when her attitude isn't what she thinks it ought to be. She doesn't always know how to handle someone so unpredictable, angry, and independent. Marion says that prayer has helped her a lot, and she is glad she has family members and close friends who support her. Nonetheless she says, "I've never had trouble with any of our five children. It's my mother . . . my mother that's so hard."

Toward Mutual Understanding

There is, unfortunately, no guarantee that parents and children will grow closer as they depend on each other more. If they develop good communication, it will suffuse the Fourth Day with a powerful sense of closeness and love, regardless of the difficulties; but if intimacy is absent, there will be an aura of fatigue and frustration surrounding all experiences, no matter how well they may work out on a practical level.

In a sense, loving communication is the one distinction families can offer. Nursing homes, after all, can provide all the practical care a person needs. Yet many people dread the thought of nursing homes. What elders need most, then, is the very thing families are particularly suited to offer—not practical care, but loving relationships. A daughter who exhausts herself cleaning Mother's apartment might help more by sitting and listening to her mother talk about her feelings.

Yet as Marion would tell us, it is not always easy to listen to older people. They live in a threatened world, and their conversation sometimes reflects it. Someone who really listens is likely to hear messages that inflict guilt. She hears, directly or indirectly, about problems that she feels powerless to change. She may hear self-pity, or meanness, or braggadocio. She may hear the same story for the fifteenth time.

Frequently the younger caregiver puts up a guard to "cut off" any unpleasant conversation. She may try to silence the older person by not responding—acting bored, growing silent. The older person usually senses this passive message, but instead of responding positively, becomes more anxious. She is likely to keep talking to reassure herself—thus perpetuating the problem.

How does one break this cycle, which may have developed over a lifetime? Though there are no guarantees, some principles may help. First, rather than giving less attention to the talkative elder, caregivers should give more—or at least, give more concentrated attention for a specific period of time. Often unpleasant behavior is a way of begging for attention. When people feel reassured and cared for, they may stop the unpleasant behavior. Though the demand for attention seems endless, it usually is not. In any case, it is better to give full, loving interest for ten minutes and then quickly leave, than to give grudging, listless attention for thirty minutes.

Hidden Meanings

A second principle is that behavior (and misbehavior) often has a hidden meaning which needs interpretation. For instance, one elderly woman in an institution broke into loud, bawdy singing whenever she was bathed until someone realized that she was intensely embarrassed at being naked in front of others.

Consider Ruby. She had her first postretirement "anger attack" when she saw the home that Leon and Marion had bought for her. Your name doesn't have to be Sigmund to realize that the timing was more than coincidental. Under the stress of her move, in which she was placing her life in Marion and Leon's hands, she was likely acting out her anxiety and fear. Similarly, after her gun went off, scaring her half to death, she must have felt insecure and incompetent. Her accusations were an overcompensation. Signing over her home brought up other internal conflicts: The idea appealed to her "sensible" side, but it made her feel vulnerable and dependent. Vulnerable people are often suspicious. They have some reason to be.

Not that "exposing" these hidden meanings to Ruby would have done the least bit of good. No one likes to be psychoanalyzed by amateurs; she would probably only have become more angry. But understanding the underlying reasons for Ruby's behavior might have made Marion feel less a personal target. She might even have been able to anticipate some of Ruby's anxiety, and assuage the worst of it in advance. It would undoubtedly have helped, too, if she had been able to get good medical attention, so she could know as far as possible whether Ruby's behavior had a physiological origin.

When you think about it in detail, you find that a great deal of stereotypical "old man's" behavior is a response to his situation. Oliver Wendell Holmes wrote: "There is one characteristic of age that strikes me more than all the physical signs, and that is the formation of habits." Indeed, many older people become glued to routines, to the annoyance of their children. But it is helpful to understand what these routines do: They protect older people from the unpredictable, and help fill every moment of the day with a kind of synthetic duty that used to be provided by career, child-rearing, or other duties.

Another stereotype of aging is pessimism. Many older people argue that the world is going to the dogs. This negativism makes them unpleasant to be with. Yet pessimism has a reason. It asserts—to a world that regards your time as lacking interest—that your time was better than theirs. Pessimism is a way of garnering some status in a world that accords elders very little.

Simone de Beauvoir writes: "Why should an old person be better than the adult or child he was? It is quite hard enough to remain a human being when everything—health, memory, possessions, standing, and authority—has been taken from you. The old person's struggle to do so has pitiable or ludicrous sides to it, and his fads, his meanness, and his deceitful ways may irritate one or make one smile; but in reality it is a very moving struggle. It is the refusal to sink below the human level, a refusal to become the insect, the inert object to which the adult world wishes to reduce the aged. There is something heroic in desiring to preserve a minimum of dignity in the midst of such total deprivation."

In assessing the "total deprivation" of the elderly, de Beauvoir was exceedingly pessimistic herself. Contrary to her words, we do at least hope, if not expect, that an older person can become better than he was. Nonetheless, she is entirely correct that a great, moving struggle for dignity and purpose, often showing itself in symbolic behavior, is common to the Fourth Day. If a father is obsessed with his garden, fussing and fuming if a neighborhood child so much as breathes on it, it helps to understand that his small patch of land is his only occupation; he may be trying to gain the same sense of achievement from it that he got from managing an office. If a mother mulls over pictures of her past, telling everyone a hundred times that she was a real beauty as a girl, it is useful to realize that she no longer feels beautiful—that, in fact, she feels her whole self-image to be fragile and threatened.

If children understand their parents in this way, or even merely *try* to understand them in this way, there will be more sympathy and less rigidity. This change of attitude can remove the barriers that often make the relationship worse. It can, in fact, make the struggle with old age meaningful and memorable for the child as well as for the parent. The relationship may not change miraculously. But it can, through difficult passages, become less a rivalry and more a comradeship.

"Engraved on my memory is one of the last conversations my wife and I had with her mother, at that time 85, sitting in her room in a nursing home. Already her eyes had degenerated so that she could barely read on some days. And she, who had been a particularly intelligent and perceptive woman in earlier years, was plagued and embarrassed by the fact that it was sometimes impossible to remember the thought with which she had started a sentence. She felt she couldn't carry on a conversation, so the fabric of her relations with others was wearing very thin. In our conversation she kept asking both of us, 'Why doesn't God take me? I'm just so useless here. There's nothing I can do anymore.' How painful it was for her to recognize this, she who had done so much for so many all her life. 'What's the purpose of my living now?' She pressed for an answer. Finally, my wife responded with, 'Well, mother, you're the oldest one in our family, perhaps you can be an example for us of how to be old—and how to die.'"

What Good Am I?

This question, asked by Arthur H. Becker's mother-in-law in his book, *Ministry with Older Persons,* is common to people who have reached the Fourth Day of old age. "What good am I?" they ask. Believers ask, "Why doesn't the Lord take me?"

People will quietly put up with considerable suffering if they see it has a point, as they may in wartime, for instance. But it is hard to see how the losses of old age serve any efficiency in God's economy. What are these losses for? Do they have any meaning? Or, more pointedly, do *I* have any meaning?

Our society understands meaningful life in terms that almost invariably fade by the Fourth Day. People are valued if their bodies are beautiful; if they have vitality, ability or brains; if they can accomplish something important. It is true enough that older people remain beautiful (in a different way), and that many famous people—Michelangelo, Leonardo da Vinci, Churchill—did some of their greatest work in their later years. But late in the Fourth Day, mentioning this begins to seem ludicrous. Should Arthur Becker have told his mother-in-law: "Remember, Mother, Churchill was elected Prime Minister in his seventies!"?

In the Fourth Day, rather than overcoming losses, older persons (and their families) are challenged to integrate loss into life. Losses no longer threaten to disrupt life; they are part of life now—constant, difficult companions. Coming to accept them requires a new understanding of life—a better one, because it is a truer one. This spiritual challenge is the "growth experience" of the Fourth Day.

The Death of Naïve Optimism

Most of us are deeply invested in an understanding of life that can hold at 40, but that fails us at 80. We see our individual selves as the whirring engine at the center of life; our prowess is the key to happiness or sadness, success or failure.

At the heart of this vision is a tremendous optimism. It holds that the world, in general, can be made a better place; and my own life, in particular, can be made lovely if I work at it. The modern pop-psychological jargon requires "taking responsibility for your life," or "owning your problems."

This makes a definite impression on the various ways people deal with old age. First, it pumps up optimism about overcoming physical losses. Read almost any publication aimed at older people and you will find encouraging information about the importance of skilled medical care, nutrition, and exercise, with the barely hidden assumption that if people would pay attention to their bodies, the losses of old age could be overcome. No one quite says that old age can be abolished, but no one quite says it can't be, either. Picture the vibrant, active, aging person, who takes megavitamins and calcium and walks three vigorous miles a day. Surely this person can never reach the point where he trembles so much he cannot get a spoon into his mouth!

But, of course, he can reach that point, and if he lives long enough, he will. Aging strips off optimism about staying vital forever.

Then comes a more sophisticated psychological approach. While not denying that old age brings physical limitations, this view sets its stock in mental victories. "Think young!" "You're only as old as you feel!" (Both statements reveal a very negative view of age.) "Stay active!"

An even more sophisticated approach speaks of a growing spirituality, serenity or esthetic appreciation that enables one to "grow old gracefully." A graceful old age is, presumably, a painless old age, in which spiritual or psychological compensations smooth out the losses. By this view, a person's spiritual awareness helps her manage life successfully, at a spiritual level if not a physical one. God is put to good use, helping us out—but we are responsible for taking charge. He acts as our all-powerful helper and friend.

If none of these approaches appeal, you can pretend that the Fourth Day has nothing to do with you personally at all. You can deal with old age strictly as an issue, discussing the needs of caregivers, rights for the disabled, Medicare benefits and housing options. The "problem" is as abstract as the "problems" of ecology or the trade imbalance. The "problem" is out there, among the species known as the elderly and the society that fails to meet their needs. The underlying feeling is that if people were better informed and more money were available from Washington, we could clean up this "old age" problem.

Each of these approaches—though they contain elements of truth—ultimately fails. Old age from the Fourth Day onward seems designed to destroy any triumphant, problem-solving approach. It is as though some evil genius had been given permission, like Satan over Job, to strip you naked. The beautiful body, protected and strengthened by cosmetics, by fashion, by exercise, by nutrition, by medicine, just quits performing, like a tired donkey one has tried to turn into a racehorse. The energy and health for money-making or career or art—whatever activities have sustained you—dissipate. One by one, your abilities are stripped away, and you must depend on others for the most elementary things—perhaps even to wash yourself. The best you can hope for is to be patronized as a former great. For what purpose do you wake each day? To burden others?

Spiritual or psychological compensations are threatened, too. Even the most graceful and spiritual old age can grow extremely ungraceful and rudely unspiritual by the Fourth Day. How much serenity is possible when you are drooling? Is acceptance merely a way to deny the obvious: that you are helpless? How do you hold despair at bay? Why be spiritual if you have no future to be spiritual for?

The attempt to treat aging impersonally, as an exercise in societal problem-solving, is also finally defeated. Problem-solving cannot cure old age because age is not a problem to be solved; it is part of life to be lived. Even in the most wonderfully beneficent society imaginable, where humane care was provided to all without cost, people would get old and suffer terrible losses.

The Fourth Day poses a riddle that modern, optimistic people cannot solve. The question is, "What good am I?" When we can't do anything, why are we here? No answer is offered by our society. People can only hope to make the best of it—to die quietly and early while they still have their health, or else to manage one last fling and then settle in for a stoic ending.

Meaning Comes from God

To solve the riddle of the Fourth Day requires that we stop thinking that life's meaning is manufactured by our energy and activity or even by our spirituality. Meaning comes from God. Whatever God has touched, whatever God loves, has value. We don't know why God should place such value on human beings, as bad as they can be. We know that God does, and that is why we can say that human life is sacred.

To accept this premise—that all life is sacred—is to see any person, including an old person who has been stripped of all her capacities, as glowing with a kind of mysterious set-apartness, a kind of holiness. She is loved by God, even on her worst days. What God has loved, we dare not disdain, whether we see what it is "good for" or not.

A Change in the Center of the Universe

Let us see whether we can explore this view more precisely. What might human worth look like, if we saw life from God's point of view? What if we shifted the center of gravity away from ourselves and our enterprising ambitions?

It is difficult for most people to even imagine this changed perspective. They assume that their way of looking at the world is the only possible way. And so even if they are Christians, the Christian perspective tends to be captured by an unchristian way of seeing. I have already described it: Spirituality becomes a way to manage a successful life. Jesus Christ helps me because he is my friend. My great concern (and presumably his) is to make me thrive. I remain at the center of the universe.

It takes quite a jolt to move from this perspective into

a truly Christian one. The shift is like one we have all been fooled by in bad movies, which tell a frightening story and then "solve the mystery" by revealing that everything was a dream. The events seemed so horrifyingly real. They *were* real, but not in the way you thought they were.

In the shift to a Christian perspective, you begin by thinking of yourself as the author of your life story. You picture it as a heroic tale with yourself as the narrator and main character. The terms are usually conventional: boy gets girl (romance), boy amasses fortune (entrepreneurial romance), boy gives all to poor (idealistic romance). Whatever the plot, you are the protagonist, and you are telling the story. But then the ground falls out from under you, and your perspective shifts. You discover that your carefully crafted story is actually a fragment of a much greater work written by someone else. In the larger work it turns out you are not the hero, but a supporting character; that you-the-writer are, in fact, an invention of a greater writer. There is another layer to reality behind the one you have been writing, and it swallows up your story. You thought you were going to make the happy ending work out through your heroic endeavor, but it turns out that, without the intervention of the real Author, there will be no happy ending at all.

The story-writer is, of course, God, and while we as characters have real, independent life (as all real characters do, even in *our* fictions), our life comes from him and will be shaped by him into his own design. He is the center of the universe. Our story can only be understood in the context of *his* story.

This change of view is the most wrenching possible, and no person on earth ever manages to make it entirely. This is because we are born with a predisposition to believe in ourselves as the sole author and hero of our story—to think of ourselves, essentially, as God. (But what a small universe this god rules!) Theologians refer to this predisposition as original sin.

Making the shift out of this predisposition can come more easily for persons who are brave enough to look closely at aging—for it is transparently obvious that old age is not, finally, a story of successful enterprise. What kind of story ends with a hero who is old, sick and dying? That is why we try to deny the reality of aging, pretending it is something that happens only to other people.

The shift will also come more easily for those who live closely with the Jewish and Christian Scriptures, for in them loss and death are a part of life that, while fearful, is ultimately redeemed by the presence of God. The Bible tells a story that includes us, and all the facts about us, including our losses, and it has a happy ending. Can we recognize ourselves in it?

In Scripture, God's love is the center of the universe; he breathes life into ours. It is from him that we get life each day, not from ourselves. Because of that, our losses and our successes are relatively less important. They matter, but they are not final and irreversible. They are not the heart of the story: Christ's life, death and resurrection are.

If Christ's resurrection is central, the ultimate loss of old age—death—is not the end of life, but a crucial turning point. After death, and only after, comes judgment, when the true meaning of each life is made clear—when all the meanings and loose endings of our brief story on earth are sorted out. After death comes glory, glory reflected from God himself. This is the biblical faith. It offers the only way I know to find meaning and hope in the Fourth Day.

The Biblical Faith

To truly make a shift of perspective requires not merely that you get the facts straight, but that you *feel* the rightness of the new perspective. It is like seeing a checkerboard as red on a black background instead of black on a red background—not a matter of explanation, but a matter of seeing it through new eyes.

To gain the perspective of the biblical faith, theological treatises may be less helpful than hearing someone at prayer who has this perspective—to see the world as he sees it before God. The psalms let us do this. They let us listen in as the very ancient people of the Old Testament prayed, for this collection was their hymnbook and their prayerbook, gradually edited over centuries, for use in their worship service. These were the songs that lasted, presumably because they became "old favorites."

I used to read the Book of Psalms, as I read all of Scripture, as a tool to help me cope. Primarily I used the psalms as mood elevators. When I was down, I read one to cheer me up. I used to find it somewhat annoying, however, that I had to skip so many of the psalms, which didn't seem very uplifting. Even some of the "best" psalms had parts that I didn't like, especially when they dwelt at length on enemies.

For these hymns are, in tone and in content, quite different from those found in our modern hymnals. They are prayers that deal with relentless trouble—slander, betrayal, anger, fear, hatred. They are anything but serene. Derek Kidner remarks that, as much as the psalms vary, they nearly all consider two realities: the active presence of a loving God, and the active presence of malevolent enemies.

The Psalms are not serene, and they are not heroic.

Human beings are not exhorted to be good or to be brave; they are typically helpless before their enemies. The Psalms leave no doubt that God must rise up, if there is to be victory. But will he? That fact is repeatedly in doubt, and some of the psalms end with the issue very much remaining in doubt. Deliverance is not automatic; problems are not solved by inserting tab A into slot B. You must ask for help, and wait helplessly, weakly. "I wait for the LORD, my soul waits, and in his word I put my hope. My soul waits for the Lord more than watchmen wait for the morning, more than watchmen wait for the morning" (130:5,6). This waiting, with its prayers for deliverance from unrelenting trouble, is a normal state of life in the Psalms.

In the New Testament, this sense of the blessedness of dependency grows, if anything, stronger. "Blessed are you who are poor," Jesus teaches, "for yours is the kingdom of God. Blessed are you who hunger now, for you will be satisfied. Blessed are you who weep now, for you will laugh." People in the Fourth Day of old age can—must—understand this point of view, in which it is the poor who will be protected by the great King, the hungry who will eat their fill, the depressed and mournful who will be overwhelmed by joy.

Jesus lived this poverty and weakness, and was found acceptable to God. In his poverty he died, yet was rescued from death. In his weakness he stumbled on his way to the cross, and later was carried away wrapped in a cloth; yet he became a channel of God's power to others. "For you know the grace of our Lord Jesus Christ, that though he was rich, yet for your sakes he became poor, so that you through his poverty might become rich" (2 Cor. 8:9).

The Christian gospel offers no hope that death and decay can be overcome by medicine, or by serene spirituality, or by societal problem-solving. Death is really death. Suffering and dependency are really awful, and inescapable. Pain and suffering are not neutral experiences, they are evil. And we have no weapons to defeat these evils. There is no hope of a happy ending to our story, so long as we write it. But since the power of God has come to earth in Jesus, who lived our story and trounced our enemies, there is a way out. He broke it open. We find it by following his path, by living intimately with him, by allowing his life to be lived through us.

Jesus willingly suffered. He willingly died. He did not conquer death by clever strategies; he conquered death by trusting his Father in heaven. He was willingly poor throughout his life, and became rich by inheritance, not by entrepreneurial skills.

The Christian anticipates joyful victory, even glory. The way to this glory is the way of the cross, however, for the simple reason that the glory never belongs to us, but can only come to us as we cling to Christ Jesus. "Therefore I will boast all the more gladly about my weaknesses, so that Christ's power may rest on me" (2 Cor. 12:9). So Paul wrote in describing God's gracious refusal to remove his "thorn." The human hero must die to himself—that is, stop being a hero. He can only gain real glory by adoring, in his weakness, the triumphant Suffering Servant.

Coming to Terms with a Hopeful Destiny

There seems to be little power or glory in the life of a woman whose eyes are failing, whose dizziness keeps her from walking, who tends with some reason toward self-pity, who is physically decaying to a slow and dreary death. Such a woman may be an extreme case, but all elders in the Fourth Day know that it is a possibility for them.

To come to terms with the Fourth Day and its losses may

be spiritually more significant than anything else a woman or man ever does. For it means coming to terms with who we really are, and what our destiny must be on this earth, and from where our strength ultimately comes. The key to that judgment is not our life's achievements, significant as they may be, but our acceptance of God's gracious love. The glory of the Fourth Day is the possibility that we be pushed out of our own hero's story, and into the freedom of Christ's.

Let us think again of Arthur Becker's mother-in-law. Where is her glory? The first and best answer is that her glory is in heaven. There is, as Scripture says, an eternal weight of glory reserved for her (2 Cor. 4:17), to be presented when she encounters Jesus face to face. So she is weak, and helpless, and dizzy, and miserable. That does not detract at all from her future. If she is one of those people going to heaven, she carries a load of glory.

Yet that does not answer the question, "What good am I now?" It might suggest that we could leap over the end of this life and land in glory. Of course, some do. Some people never seem to suffer; they end their lives quietly without much sickness. But for those who do suffer, the point of their life is clear: their weakness can serve as a means of spiritual growth, preparing them (and those around them) for heaven. Indeed, the sufferers may need growth lessons less than those who watch them, helping and serving them. As Arthur Becker's wife said, "Mother . . . perhaps you can be an example for us of how to be old—and how to die."

Paul wrote, "We rejoice in the hope of the glory of God [i.e. heaven]. *Not only so,* but we also rejoice in our sufferings" (Rom. 5:2,3, italics mine). That is because sufferings make us poor so that we can be blessed. Sufferings strip away earthly resources so that we have hands free to hold heavenly riches. They destroy our old view of our heroism so that we can grasp the new. Nobody seems less like a hero than an old, dependent person. Yet for that very reason, he or she may become far more prepared to welcome a true hero, a Savior.

As Paul went on to tell the Romans, "We rejoice in our sufferings, because we know that suffering produces perseverance; perseverance, character; and character, hope." Perseverance in the Bible is not just "hanging in there"; it is based on trust in God's active and persistent love. Similarly, biblical character is not rugged individualism; it is consistency in responding to difficult situations with faith in God. "God, I don't understand what you are doing or why, but I trust you."

If we develop character, it leads us to hope, for God does not desert those who lean on him. "And hope does not disappoint us, because God has poured out his love into our hearts by the Holy Spirit, whom he has given us" (5:5) Hope, for the Christian, rests in one certainty: Jesus. Ultimately we will see him in heaven. Here and now we can receive a deposit of his love, when we are given the Holy Spirit. In the Spirit we meet Jesus, and his love pours out into our hearts. This love spills over us to others.

"Why doesn't God take me? Why am I here?" You are here to experience love, receiving it and also giving it. Everything that God asks and expects of us can be summed up in this: Love God, and love your neighbor.

What Love Requires

Love takes no competence. It does not require heroic endeavor. It can be done by anyone in any condition, so long as they have stopped being wrapped up in themselves. Someone who is paralyzed can love with her eyes. Someone who is blind can love with his voice and his touch. Only this is required: To love your neighbor or to love God, you must make the shift away from yourself as center of the universe. You must take God's (or your neighbor's) life story for your own.

You can find people in every nursing home who do this, making an impact through their love. They give their lives to others. They breathe out love. The contribution may seem puny. But Jesus intended to impress on his disciples that God judges our giving by percentage, not gross total. The widow's two cents weigh the scales more heavily than the piled-up gifts of the rich. This is one way in which the poor are blessed: they can much more easily give their all.

We are God's chosen, not to make us strong, but to confound the strong. "God chose the weak things of the world to shame the strong. He chose the lowly things of this world and the despised things—and the things that are not—to nullify the things that are, *so that no one may boast before him*" (1 Cor. 1:27–29). Simply to be God's children is power and glory. You cannot witness to his grace and love except as someone who remains weak. The elderly in the Fourth Day are often especially graced and loved this way.

That is why some become so good at praying for others. What is intercessory prayer, except a persistent confession that you are helpless? That you can't do all that is needed; you must appeal to God for mercy toward yourself and others?

The elderly living in the Fourth Day cannot go out to do great things. They cannot beat their losses. They cannot even be perfectly serene. They can only demonstrate the confounding power of God's choosing the weak. They can witness to their increasing faith in him as all other "faiths" get stripped away. They can love. They can pray. They can give their all. If they manage to do these things, not perfectly but substantially, the Fourth Day will be truly a growth experience.

I saw this at work in my grandfather. He could not speak in the last years of his life, and his uselessness lay heavy on him—he had always been an impatient man. But people in the small Kansas farm town where he lived, people not given to sentimentality, loved him because of what showed on his face.

He was always in church, and something you saw made your heart glow. I cannot explain it, though I felt it, and I know others felt it too. "He has so much love," people said.

Once someone took him to a faith healer, in hopes that his aphasia would be healed. My grandfather was no Pentecostal, but he went forward to be prayed for. The healer balked. He would pray with my grandfather as a brother, he said, but not for healing. He said that my grandfather was already in the condition God wanted him to be.

The Fourth Day: A Practical Checklist

From such exalted talk, I want to return to some practical considerations. In the Fourth Day there is no point in denying the reality of dependency. Far better is to seek a creative adaptation to dependency, and to prepare well for more. There is a strong tendency to put off change until a crisis necessitates it. It is far better to move aggressively and early. Following is a mixed bag of practical suggestions:

Age-proof the house. Just as parents of young children "child-proof" their home, so elderly people should "age-proof" their dwelling. Steep stairs, "step-ups," curving pathways, low shrubbery or potted plants should be eliminated if at all possible. Grab-bars can be attached to critical spots—the bathroom, particularly. Telephones should be located conveniently, especially in the bedroom.

Take driving lessons. The ability to drive is, in most of America, a key to independence. There is controversy over whether older drivers are more dangerous than younger drivers. They have no more accidents, it seems, but then they usually don't drive as much. Whatever the ultimate conclusion to this debate, many older people will feel nervous about their driving, and many of their children will worry for them. These worries often make people give up driving sooner than they need to. Driving lessons especially designed for older people can help settle fear, strengthen latent skills, and offer objective guidance on whether driving is still reasonably safe.

Establish a nutritional diet. Older people, particularly if they live alone, fairly often suffer from malnutrition. With all their other losses, they cannot afford to add this unnecessary loss.

Most towns and cities offer Meals on Wheels, an organization which delivers balanced meals to the door. Even better, in some cases, are senior dining rooms, where a good meal is available daily. Elders may be more inclined to eat in the company of others. Eating regular meals with children or near neighbors is another solution. Though I blanch to say it, TV dinners might be a consideration: They can be nutritionally balanced, and are easy to prepare. Diet is a very personal matter, and any change in eating patterns requires an adjustment. It is a good idea to begin these adjustments long before a crisis.

Think through good routines and habits. Habits help enormously when trouble comes. They keep us doing what we should even when we feel overwhelmed. They also prevent a great many disasters. For instance, many caregivers call their aging parents each morning at a certain time to check on them. Routines may include starting every visit with a cup of tea and some conversation, or taking a Sunday afternoon drive. Old people are creatures of habit because so much else is being jerked out from under their feet. Habits provide a sense of stability.

Develop good foot care. Though this suggestion may seem trivial, competent foot care is often extremely important to elderly people. Because their circulation tends to be poor, minor sores can fester. Toenails often grow thick and horny and require special tools for cutting. Feet that hurt make life miserable; and pain in walking leads to isolation and increased dependency.

Learn some compensating tricks. Depending upon an older person's disabilities, there are many tricks that can be used to maintain an independent lifestyle. For instance, those with failing eyesight can identify medicine bottles or salt shakers if various shaped pieces of felt are glued to them. A social worker or other caring professional can often suggest possibilities that solve, simply and conveniently, other such knotty problems.

Find competent, reliable help. This is particularly critical for seniors who wish to stay in their home, or even in their children's home, indefinitely. Help with cooking, washing, cleaning, and companionship is needed, but such help is certainly expensive; and there are tremendous frustrations involved in finding cheerful, capable people to do it. If you can manage such care, however, it lifts a great deal of stress from the main caregiver; and this can enable an "at-home" situation to last much longer.

One of the most difficult issues is what happens when the hired caregiver is sick or wants to go on vacation . . . or quits, or proves unsatisfactory. If no backup is available, the end result can be more stress, not less. The best solution, say many experienced people, is an agency that guarantees a replacement helper, and will deal with hiring, firing and disciplinary matters for you. Agencies are usually more expensive, of course. At the very least, during the Fourth day, you should learn what your options are and, if possible, try them out.

Have your first family conference. It's true that one family member usually carries the brunt of responsibility. But it's also true that this situation often breeds misunderstandings. The main caregiver may feel that no other family members are concerned; the other family members may feel that the main caregiver won't take advice or help.

The solution is a family council, in which all concerned family members participate. In addition, it may be helpful to invite an outsider—a pastor, a doctor, a trusted friend, or a social worker—to facilitate the discussion.

Many such family councils convene for the first time when faced by an imminent decision—typically, whether Mom or Dad ought to be in a nursing home. It would be helpful to have such a council long before drastic decisions are necessary. A meeting simply to hear Mom out on what kind of care she would prefer is good; all of the children will probably want to hear her views on that sooner or later. Launching the family council early simply means that the vehicle is primed and ready for communication during a time of genuine crisis.

Find out what social services are available. Perhaps the easiest method is to locate a social worker who specializes in geriatrics and will take private cases. Such trained counselors are especially useful for those trying to provide care for a parent living some distance away. Unfortunately, there are few such specialists, and they usually must charge for their services. The only alternative is to find out for yourself what's available.

The best place to start is your Area Agency on Aging

(which may go by another name, such as County Council on Aging). After that, you simply have to start calling. Here is a brief listing of where to look in your telephone book:

In the white pages:
• Council on Aging
• Community Service Society
• Catholic Charities Family and Community Service (you need not be Catholic)
• Family Service Agency
• Jewish Family and Community Services (you need not be Jewish)
• Protestant Federation of Welfare Agencies (you can also check each denomination: Episcopal, Lutheran, Baptist, etc.)
• Salvation Army
• American Red Cross
• Volunteers of America
• Mental Health Association
• Legal Aid (for legal assistance)

In the yellow pages:
• Health and Welfare agencies
• Home Health Care
• Homes-Residential Care
• Nursing Homes
• Nursing Services
• Retirement and Life Care Communities
• Senior Citizens' Service Organizations
• Social Service Agencies
• Social Workers

In city, county, state and federal listings:
• Commission on Aging
• Department of Community Service
• Department of Health
• Department of Housing and Community Development
• Department of Human Resources
• Department of Social Services
• Department of Welfare

It is, by unanimous testimony, a confusing, constantly changing network of social agencies. However, part of the reason for this is the number of services available. Although more can be done, our country has made a substantial, sustained effort to help the elderly.

Unfortunately, many caregivers do not know about the help that is available. By the time they realize they need help, they are often in no condition to run the maze of social agencies. It is difficult, no doubt, to make yourself investigate services that you hope you will never need. But the earlier you can do so, the more naturally you will be able to adjust to growing dependency. What usually limits a parent's independence, ultimately, is the exhausted resources of caregivers.

Ask the church to help. I would be remiss if I merely pointed toward social service organizations. Many of the needs of elderly people do not demand highly skilled or experienced people. They can be filled by ordinary people willing to give their time and attention to visiting, fixing meals, cleaning, companionship, drives in the country, gardening, fix-it, and day care. Unfortunately, once elderly people are unable to leave their homes, they fade from the attention of their churches. Also unfortunately, their children often never think to ask the church directly for help. I suspect many churches would be willing to offer help, if they knew what was needed.

DAY 5

❧

MEMO TO MY MOTHER:

I AM THANKFUL THAT YOU HAVE BEEN QUITE frank with us about caring for Grandpa. It must have been tempting to brush the indignities of his last years into the background and focus on his bravery and suffering. However, he was a very stubborn man, sure of himself to the brink of tyranny. That pervaded those years as much as his goodness and greatness. So you have told me.

Now it is easier to laugh about it. You told us, during this last visit, about the occasion when you had cleaned up his spills and changed his bedding seven times in a single day, and then he took it into his mind to urinate in the general direction of the toilet from the doorway, because he didn't have time or patience to get nearer. "He couldn't have done that even as a very young man," you laughed, "let alone in his eighties." Oh, you were angry with him that day, you told us. You said you could have killed him.

I gather that the two of you did battle quite often. And I am

179

beginning to understand, a bit, the intensity you put into his care. You still speak with a certain stress of outrage about the doctors who botched his case after cataract surgery—doctors who couldn't make the time to answer questions, doctors who acted as though it was inevitable that old people would react violently to their medicine, doctors who, though most of their patients were old, still had only one bathroom in their office, reached by a narrow, steep stairway.

I understand that it was no lark—that it was, as you have told us, distasteful to clean your father's privates, galling to conquer and reconquer his stubbornness, heartbreaking to watch him suffer. And yet, strangely, I cannot support any real horror over it, perhaps because I don't sense you do either. It all seems fitting: grave, tragic, turbulent, tragicomic—"fitting" that a great man (or any man or woman with God's greatness in him or her) leave us only after a struggle. Paint it in dark colors: a Rembrandt.

It does not stick in my mind as a shattering contradiction to a good life. The enduring portrait is of an appropriate end: an old man leaning (and pressing) on a strong adult daughter, taking strength from (and pushing against) one to whom he had given strength; the two locked together both in embrace and hammer lock until the end. So often the ties between parents and children have this struggling ambivalence. I am reminded of Jacob wrestling with God, and saying, "I will not let you go unless you bless me."

And you—in the end, were you blessed? I think you were.

The Fifth Day: Dependency

CELIA KNEW THAT LIFE IS DIFFICULT—HAD known it since her husband, a farmer, died without warning in the deepest part of the Depression, leaving her with six children. Yet Celia was a woman who knew how to make the best of things. She was cheerful and full of humor, and she had plenty of friends. Her relatives offered to take care of some of the children, but rather than split up the family, she moved them all into a smaller house—practically a shack—and took in laundry and sewing. The grocery man in their small Montana town was kind enough to let them run up a bill. Even so, often enough they had only oatmeal to eat, with milk from the cows, which the children milked.

Celia had a little pump organ that she played by ear. There was a CCC camp nearby, and sometimes some of the boys would visit, do some chores, share a meal, and sing. They called her Mother Murphy, and she kept in touch with some of them for years after. Celia also took in two grandnieces and some poor farm boys.

During the war, Celia got a job cooking at a state institution, where she worked until she retired. Then she moved to the state of Washington to be near a daughter who was divorced and bringing up her children alone. Celia bought a house within walking distance. As always, she made friends quickly and became active in a local church.

When she reached her early seventies, Celia decided that she wanted to move back to her old home in Montana, where many of her children still lived. But she had always dreamed of seeing Alaska and taking a cruise on the Inland Passage. One of her sons drove her and her older sister to Vancouver, and they boarded a ship there. But Celia fell on the boat and broke her hip. She was evacuated by air to Vancouver; then, once her condition had stabilized, she was flown to a hospital in Montana. But she never walked again.

Her spirits didn't flag for long. She moved into a retirement center, where she had her own apartment and meals were provided. Often she said to her children, who saw her often, "If this had to happen, I'm glad it happened on the way home." After five years she needed a hip operation. While recovering, she moved into a nursing home, being too independent to want to live with any of her children. She wheeled around cheerfully, made friends, and joined in the activities. Her son took care of her finances, and the other children visited often, took her out for rides, and had her in their homes for meals.

Toward the end Celia's eyesight failed her, and she could not read. Her daughter Rose went to see her every day, but the visits grew difficult. Rose was a sensitive person who became disturbed when Celia was cranky. The nursing home personnel suggested to Rose that she not come every day, but she persisted, except when other brothers and sisters could spell her.

Then Rose's husband Con died suddenly. Celia had been very fond of Con, and she reacted with great sadness. She would say, "Why couldn't it have been me?" Celia seemed to lose interest in life, and thirty days after Con's death, she joined him.

Dependence Is Here to Stay

Celia's story, with its tone of cheer, is as typical of the Fifth Day as the more frightening image projected by, say, an Alzheimer's victim. Celia had "made do" all her life, and so she did to the end. There were some hard times, especially in the last month of her life, but she left behind a strong legacy of cheer. Many elders do. That's important to remember, because the Fifth Day—Dependence Day— is usually hard on everyone, even if they react as well as Celia and her family.

What separates the Fifth Day from the Fourth—Role Reversal Day? In the Fifth Day, a senior moves from partial, sporadic dependence to a far more general and daily need for help. Sometimes one dramatic episode makes the difference overnight: typically, a stroke or a bad fall. More often, however, the Fourth Day merges gradually into the Fifth Day, dependency growing imperceptibly. There may be a long period of oscillation between partial and full dependency—a month of recovery from a fall, followed by two months of limited independence, followed by two weeks in bed with influenza, and so on.

In the Fourth Day, the most important concern is role reversal. Parents and children rework their relationship.

Children learn to help without dominating; parents learn to accept help and deal with their fears of being a burden to their children.

In the Fifth Day, that psychological battle gradually peters out. Dependency becomes a more or less accepted reality. The focus of attention shifts to practical decisions of caregiving. Who will provide care, and where, and how?

Some of the concerns introduced by the Fourth Day grow much larger. For caregivers, this is a period dogged by exhaustion. Almost always they feel that more is required of them than they can give. For those receiving so much care, there is frequently a problem of depression, of "giving up." After all, their worst fear—becoming a burden—has come true. They face daily indignities—being wiped and washed and pushed and fed. If they are in a nursing home, they are surrounded by those who display the other great fear—losing your mind. The questions, "Why am I here?" and "Why doesn't the Lord take me?" grow in frequency and intensity. The suicide rate is high. Though the elderly make up only 11 percent of the population, they account for one-fourth of all suicides. Whenever an older person mentions suicide, he needs to be taken seriously.

The Fifth Day is no fun for anybody. However, it rarely lasts long. Often the Fifth Day is measured in months rather than years. When this stage is extended longer—as it is for Alzheimer's victims, for example—caregivers are very often stretched to the breaking point.

Ben and Maria lived in their own home into their late seventies. Neither one had experienced serious health difficulties. They were close to their three children— Ben, Fran, and Maxine.

At nine o'clock one Sunday evening, Fran called his sister Maxine with shocking news. Their mother had died suddenly half an hour earlier. She had been sick all week, but had seemed to be recovering. The death took everyone completely by surprise.

So Maria, at 78, escaped the Fifth Day entirely. She had taught an older ladies' Sunday school class, and had spent hours visiting members as, one by one, they had entered rest homes. Seeing them, she had dreaded the same fate for herself. Instead, she had remained active, independent, and happy to the end of her life.

This was not to be the case for her husband Ben. He continued to work part-time until he was 82, and stayed in the family home. But the house became too much for him to manage. Besides, it carried too many reminders of Maria. So he moved into a one-bedroom, federally-subsidized apartment for seniors. Every night he went to his son's house for dinner. When Fran and his family were away, they left a casserole so that Ben would have at least one good meal a day.

He had a small stroke, but recovered fully. Then one day, when Fran called him, the phone rang for a long time before Ben answered. When he did, he was mumbling. His son raced over and found Ben on the floor. The apartment was stifling: The oven was on at 450 degrees, and a chicken pie had been reduced to charcoal.

Ben had suffered a stroke, and he was mentally confused. He stayed in the hospital for a long time. As he recovered his health, Ben talked about going home. He wanted out of the hospital and back into his cozy apartment. But the doctor said he would require 24-hour nursing care, which would be extremely expensive.

Another option was for one of the children to invite him into their home. But was that workable? Ben was the kind of man who dreaded bothering anybody. He had always said that he wouldn't live with any of his kids; he'd go to the "Old Soldier's Home" first. They weren't sure how much weight to give that now. Other factors were clearly against inviting him in. Fran and his wife both worked, as did Ben, Jr., and his wife. Maxine's house had stairs, and her community had no Veteran's hospital nearby.

The only other option was the nursing home.

For almost two decades Ben had lived an extremely vigorous and happy retirement. In all that time, his close, loving family had never seriously discussed with him or each other what kind of care would be desirable in case of disability. They had let pass his "Old Soldier's Home" comment. It had been hard to imagine his facing these kinds of choices.

Options in Caring for Dependent Elders

Ben's story is somewhat typical of the Fifth Day. All the experts (and simple common sense) dictate that a family should discuss these matters long in advance. Yet when the day comes, many families feel unprepared.

The National Health Survey taken in 1977 tried to assess dependency for older people. Considering dependency in the activities of daily living—bathing, dressing, eating, and toileting—they found this pattern by age groups:

65–74	3.5% dependent
75–84	11% dependent
85 +	35% dependent

A person in his late sixties is, therefore, likely to be 20 years away from this issue—as far removed as someone in college from the crisis of her fortieth birthday. It is difficult to prepare for something that distant and uncertain. As the years go by—and change is imperceptibly slow—it is easy to put off serious planning.

Still, millions of Americans are heavily dependent on others for their care. And there are fewer people available to care for them. In 1900, there were about eight Americans aged 18 to 59 for every one over 60; by 1980, the ratio was 3 ½ to one; and by 2030, the ratio is projected to become two to one. The ratio of 80-year-olds to younger people is growing even faster. The odds are increasing that you will have to deal with the kind of choice Ben and his children faced: What kind of care does your aging parent need? There are not too many options. These are the major four:

Independent living. With an increasing range of at-home services available, some heavily dependent seniors are able to stay in their own homes. With enough money, anything is possible. What usually eliminates this option, ultimately, is finances. Full-time skilled nursing care is beyond most people's budgets. Therefore, experts usually concentrate on developing a care network that will *extend* elders' stay in their own homes. A care network might combine the Meals on Wheels program, regular visits from a nurse, a housecleaner, and a church volunteer who helps once a month with finances. Appropriate aid can often give elders one, two, three, or more extra years in the privacy and familiarity of their homes.

Sharing a home with children usually relies on the same network of care, but with children on site to manage it, and to do much of the work. An elder may have his own separate apartment within the home, or may (at the other extreme) share a bedroom with a grandchild. Usually, some modest physical modifications are necessary if the elder is truly dependent—ramps and railings, particularly. If the feasibility of independent living in the Fifth Day depends largely on money, sharing a home depends largely on the personalities of those involved.

Residential Care Homes (also called Foster Care or Group Care) are approximately what most nursing homes used to be before they added the dimension of medical assistance. They often house fewer than a dozen people, and are run by a family. The quality of care depends a great deal on the people involved. Residential care homes cannot provide the skilled medical attention offered by nursing homes, but they may be a great deal more like "home." And, they are usually less expensive.

Nursing Homes are familiar to all, yet often feared and reviled. Nursing homes do have their problems, but the public perception is out of kilter with reality in most cases. People blame the institutions rather than face the possibility that there may be no escape from the radical losses of the Fifth Day. Nearly everyone who works with older people concedes that nursing homes are necessary, and that most people who are in them need to be there. Most will also admit that, while there are bad nursing homes, good ones are at least as common. If nursing homes disappeared, we would have to reinvent them. Still, not many people find them pleasant places.

Day Activities Centers are a fairly recent innovation. They particularly assist families that want to share a home with an elder, but are unable to be present during the day. Someone who works can drop off an elder in the morning and pick him up at the end of the day, knowing that the social environment will be stimulating and helpful. Day Centers also offer "respite" for caregivers who need an occasional day off.

The Pros and Cons of Institutions

Contrary to much popular wisdom, there has been no discernible increase in the tendency to institutionalize older people. Since taxpayers often end up footing the bill, many states have set up agencies to ensure that no one on Medicaid enters a nursing home without requiring its care. The number of people in American nursing homes has been increasing at about the same speed that the number of "old old" people has been growing. That doesn't sound alarming until you consider that the population of the "old old" is growing at a remarkable rate. Projections suggest a need to increase nursing home beds by at least 50 percent in the next twenty years. Since launching new nursing homes is generally expensive and time-consuming, we can probably anticipate shortages of space—and bigger bills.

Meanwhile, the number of elders living with their kids has dropped precipitously. For instance, in 1960, three out of five widows over 75 lived with their children; by 1980, only about one of three. People often regard this as a symbol of extended family breakdown, and thus of the callous coldness of modern American society. (In Japan, by contrast, well over two-thirds of *all* elders live with their children.) But more likely, it's a sign of increased financial independence. In all surveys, older people indicate overwhelmingly that they do not want to live with their children. With Social Security and better pension plans, most can afford not to—at least until they reach the Fifth Day and become too dependent to live alone. Then they may be faced with the choice of living with their kids or entering a nursing home. Some will move in with their children, but generally not because they are delighted by the family values that choice represents. (People in Japan may value their extended family more than we do, but no doubt the extraordinarily high cost of housing also affects their choice.)

In the abstract, it is possible to argue heatedly about the value of various housing choices. In practice, "right" and "wrong" are blurred. Most seniors will stay in their homes as long as they (or their children) think they can. Many will have a stint, sometimes a long stint, living with children. Many of these will eventually move to a nursing home. The key concerns are those of timing and circumstance: *How* can the needs of 16-year-old Joe be balanced with those of his grandmother? *How many* falls should a senior take before being considered unsafe in his own home?

When is a nursing home necessary? Unfortunately, there are no neat answers.

Making the Decision as a Family

Decisions about where to live are hard to undo once they are made. In a move, possessions and furniture that "make a house a home" may be sold or given away. A familiar and beloved house, apartment, or room may be sold or rented to another person. And the move itself puts heavy stress on older people; they may, by the Fifth Day, be too weak to make another move if the first one doesn't work out.

Because of the quasi-permanence of these decisions, it's particularly valuable to make them in a family conference. A family conference ought to be a reasonably formal proceeding, with a clear, agreed-upon agenda, and an orderly way for everyone to speak his mind. A family conference ensures that the senior, who is most affected, is heard; that all important information is presented; and that all relatives who are involved participate in the decision. For the primary caregiver, who lives day-to-day with the needs of a parent, a meeting like this may seem unnecessary. However, because resentments are quite common when others feel left out of a decision, the results will be well worth any special arrangements that must be made.

If the elder concerned is mentally confused, it may be difficult to know exactly what preferences she has—or even whether she has any preferences. Those with experience caution, however, that often the elder knows what she wants, even though she can't express herself clearly. That's one reason why a family conference often works better with an experienced outside facilitator present. That person can make sure that everyone's opinion, particularly the opinion of the elder, is heard. Many Area Agencies on Aging have such facilitators available without cost.

There are practical and legal considerations involved in housing decisions, so it's often necessary to discuss some kind of legal authority for the person who will be in charge of making arrangements. The choices have been discussed briefly, beginning on page 61. At the very least, you need to set up a joint bank account. Most people say it's well worth the time and money to consult a lawyer about the many varying forms of living trusts and durable powers of attorney. If these have not been arranged long in advance, now is the time.

Sometimes, if a senior is unwilling or unable to grant anyone else authority to make decisions for him, it is necessary to go to the courts to seek a guardianship. This is a grave decision, for in declaring an elder "mentally incompetent," the court effectively strips him of all adult rights. The situation can easily be abused by an unscrupulous or careless guardian. Sometimes, however, there is no alternative. Each state, and sometimes each county, handles procedures for guardians differently. Some time is usually required to obtain a guardianship through the courts, even though in most places it is perhaps a too-routine procedure. Once again, a lawyer with experience in these kinds of cases should be consulted. Many Area Agencies on Aging provide free legal advice.

Carol was six years old when her maternal grandfather "came for a visit and stayed for 25 years." No living arrangements or ground rules had been discussed ahead of time. Since another daughter had asked him to leave her house, Carol's mother felt she couldn't turn him out—he had nowhere else to go.

A little girl has ideas about what grandparents should be. Carol recalls a vague, dull disappointment when he didn't turn out to be the kind of grandfather she had imagined. She has no memory of ever sitting on his lap. He was a loner, seemingly disinterested in life. When the family included him in their vacation plans, he asked constantly when they would return home. If he didn't go along on the trip, he complained, "You never take me anywhere." Financially, he made no contribution toward the expenses of his care; he never even remembered his daughter's birthday.

He did try to help in his own way, but it often caused frustration. He would run the dishwasher with only three dishes inside, or damage clothes by washing them improperly. Though Carol's mother asked him not to do these things, he persisted until she gave up telling him.

Twenty years after Carol's grandfather moved in, her grandmother decided to do the same thing. The two had divorced long ago, when Carol's mother was a child. Carol and her sisters, now grown, opposed this arrangement; they felt their mother, though a strong personality, had been under enough stress and they feared the worst.

As it turned out, Grandmother did antagonize her ex-husband over petty things. But she, while difficult, also had a good sense of humor and brought life into the home more than she drained it away. Because of her advanced osteoporosis, she spent much of her time in her bedroom, yet entered, as much as pain would allow, into relationship with the rest of the family. Sensitive to financial concerns, she insisted on helping.

During the last few years of his life, Carol's grandfather grew senile. For the last year or so, he couldn't be left alone. He would start fires in garbage cans. Sometimes he saw boats in the field outside the house. Meanwhile, Carol's grandmother needed constant attention. She couldn't get out of bed without help, and she was frightened of dying alone. That final period was very wearing on Carol's mother. It let up only when the former husband and wife died, at home, within six months of each other.

Sharing a Home

Studies indicate that Americans feel a growing optimism about sharing their home with older parents. This optimism tends to diminish, however, the more experience a person has with such intergenerational living. Carol's story illustrates why.

Many contemporary elders grew up with grandparents in the home and are quite certain they do not want to duplicate that experience. They value their own privacy and independence, and they do not want to burden their children, even though they hear their children saying that it will be no burden. They think they know better. Having listened to a number of people who have cared for parents or grandparents in their home, I now think my elders *do* know better.

In any case, as Dean Black has written, "An older person who feels he is being a burden will be miserable whether he is actually being a burden or not."

I emphasize this point because I have noticed how often younger people assume that the best, the most moral, and most beneficial choice will always be cogenerational living. I myself certainly made that assumption. And while virtually every ethnic group smugly asserts, "We take care of our old people," Simone de Beauvoir, after a wide survey of the anthropological literature, sums it up this way: "The most usual choice of communities with inadequate resources, whether they are agricultural or nomadic, is to sacrifice the old."

Our assumptions, then, don't always match up with experience. Sharing a home is an option, but it certainly should not be considered the only good option.

The Independent Ideal

If there is any ideal to strive for, it is independent living. People want to live the way they have grown accustomed to living—in their own home, surrounded by their own things, answering to no one. A child who supports this kind of lifestyle will not necessarily give any less than one who invites his parent into his own home.

"I spend all my time taking care of my father," a Chicago woman who lives a twenty-minute drive from her father's house told Otten and Shelley. "I do his marketing and most of his cooking. Someone comes in every morning to help him get bathed and dressed, to fix his breakfast and do a little housecleaning. But I have to check to see if she's there every day, and if she isn't, I have to go over myself. A bus comes to take him to the clinic and the doctor. He can still go to sit on the park bench, but there is no bus to the part of town where his two friends live, and I have to drive him there. When I'm not with him, he's on the telephone, wanting to know when I'll be over. He may not be ready for a nursing home, but I sure am!"

If independent living is ideal, what makes older people move out of their homes? Here are a number of the most common reasons:

- The hospital discharges them before they are ready to care for themselves. It seems easier—at least it takes less planning—to have them stay with a child than to go back into their own homes.
- The elder becomes accident-prone—leaving on the gas, forgetting something in the oven, neglecting to lock the doors, and most commonly, falling. Children worry that their parents will do themselves real harm, and that no one will know until hours later.

- Having lost a spouse, an elder may find the old home place holds too many memories and moves in with a child for companionship.
- The care network needed to ensure that an elder can stay at home is not available in that community.
- Living with a child is less expensive than living alone.

All these are valid reasons, but some can be overcome if there is conviction that they *should* be overcome. Unfortunately, children often don't grasp the importance of a parent's home. They forget that a home is a symbol of independence, and that the way a person arranges his belongings and decorates his space is as personal as the clothes he wears. When a person moves in with someone else, he sacrifices some of himself.

Safety is certainly a significant issue for older, dependent people who live alone, but safety is only one factor that should be balanced against others. The horrible possibility of someone falling and lying helplessly in pain for hours, unable to summon help, must be balanced against other horrible possibilities, such as a protracted death in a nursing home, or a really miserable co-residence. Risk of death and suffering are inevitable in the Fifth Day; they are not absolute justification for action.

Making a Shared Home Work

While I have made a point of emphasizing the negative experience of many people who share a home with their parents, I must also point out that many families simply wouldn't have it any other way. Family togetherness is critically important to them, and they value the family history and the committed love that sharing a home represents. Carol, who lived with her divorced grandparents as a child, looks back with great appreciation. "As a small girl I remember my mother telling me, 'Grandmother's going to sweep the floor, and she probably won't do a very good job. But don't say anything to her. We'll leave it because she needs to feel like she's helping.'" Carol also learned an important lesson about love. "I felt guilty for not having warm, fuzzy feelings for my grandfather. But I came to realize I could have those and still be a terrible granddaughter if I never did anything to add to his life."

People who have shared a home unfailingly emphasize the importance of privacy. But some of these concerns diminish when an elder reaches a state of high dependence. If Grandmother is in bed most of the time, or can't remember what happened ten minutes ago, issues like privacy all but disappear. Other issues, however, loom larger, particularly the amount of care needed. Again, it's extremely important that the whole family understand who is responsible for what aspect of the care, and that the primary caregiver be relieved of other responsibilities.

A highly dependent elder changes the house he enters. Physical modifications should be considered, such as tearing out carpet. Wheelchair ramps may be installed, though this need not be an expensive proposition: With two-by-fours and half-inch plywood, a hammer, nails, and saw, it is possible to manufacture something that will work adequately. A medical supply store will be able to show you an impressive array of equipment for rental or purchase: railings, hydraulic lifts for the bath, "trapezes" to help a bedridden person sit up, grab bars for the bathroom, wheelchairs in hundreds of designs and models, hospital beds, portable commodes. The cost of many of these devices is covered by Medicare.

You probably don't like the idea of turning your house into a hospital. But it's often part of the reality of living with a highly dependent person. Such devices are meant to help, and they do. Other realities can't be resolved so easily—spills and stains, nicked and bruised furniture and walls, falls and accidents and unpleasant odors. None of it will kill you. But it is a good idea to be aware of what's involved before you begin. This is what parents mean, in part, when they talk about "being a burden."

You would never dream, if you met Sally, that she has any eccentricity in her genes. Sally is a thoroughly conservative person. But shortly before WWII began, Sally's father, an independent soul, joined Mankind United, a utopian commune that was flourishing on the West Coast. He and his amenable wife moved to San Francisco, giving up all their possessions.

Sally and her husband Grey went on living in the family house for several years after that, making payments. Then one day a woman came to the door, identifying herself as a representative of Mankind United and ordering them out of the house within the next two weeks. They were to leave every stick of furniture behind.

Sally contacted the FBI to see if anything could be done, but failing to find assistance there, she and Grey moved to a rented house. Sally's father was no help, either. He took the view that they should join the organization as he had.

Mankind United moved Sally's parents from one location to another up and down the coast. They worked in various businesses that the commune had started, and stood in line to eat communal meals. For many years they almost lost contact with Sally. "Mother married Dad for better or for worse," Sally explains, "and sometimes it was a lot worse."

After more than a decade of utopia, the dream wore thin. Sally began to receive more communication from her parents. She wrote back, telling them that, if they ever wanted to get out, they would be welcome in her home.

One day in the late fifties, her parents appeared on the doorstep. They owned absolutely nothing. They stayed with Sally and Grey for about a month until they were old enough for Social Security; then they moved into a little duplex. The radical communal life having failed them, they were able to fall back on other more familiar forms of communal life: family and government.

When Sally's mother died, her father moved in again. He had not become any easier to get along with. "He always told people that he had come to live with us and take care of us," she said. And in his own mind, that was a fact. He could still drive, and he would take off without telling anyone where he was going. What worried Sally most, though, was his tendency to turn on the gas stove and forget about it.

The living arrangement, while far from ideal, worked adequately until Sally's husband became extremely ill. Twice, Grey caught pneumonia, and he was finally diagnosed as having pleural fibrosis. He would never work again. Fortunately, he had just completed 25 years as a carpenter and was eligible for a union pension. Nonetheless, Sally had to return to work as a dental assistant.

For a time their son took over household duties. Grey could only sit in his chair and watch. Sally remembers her father being very unpleasant. "He was planning shenanigans of all kinds. You had to keep an eye on him."

Sally's sister, who lived in a nearby town, refused to take her father in, and while a brother in Colorado was willing, her father wouldn't agree to stay with him. Sally could see only one other choice: a rest home. She does not think that she would ever have put her father in a rest home had Grey not been sick.

With the decision made, however, she called her sister. "Look, kid, this is your responsibility too." Together they took their father to look at the options open to him. But he resisted stubbornly. "I'm just not going to leave. This is my home." They took him anyway.

One rest home was run by a very likeable older woman who kept a handful of men in a big, Victorian house near the center of town. Both sisters liked her immediately. They made the arrangements, but were unsure how their father would respond.

The next morning Sally left for work. Her sister packed a suitcase for her father, took it to the car, and told him, "We're ready to go." He went quietly.

"He made a pretty good adjustment," Sally said. "He would walk around town and talk to anybody who would listen. I think he gave away or was conned out of the few possessions he had, because when we moved him, he had nothing left." Sally visited him often.

As the years passed, he lost touch with reality; sometimes he recognized Sally and sometimes not. Seeing that he might not live much longer, she wrote her brother in Colorado to come for a visit.

The first day of the visit, Sally's father greeted his son. "I understand you came from Colorado. Isn't that a coincidence. I have a son in Colorado." The son's face fell. Later Sally's brother told her, "Sis, we never believed what you told us until we saw it for ourselves."

Later that summer Sally moved her father to a nursing home for closer medical attention. Two days after his arrival, however, he died quite suddenly.

Sally is a serious and thoughtful person. "It's always been my prayer," she says, "that my children will never have to care for us as we cared for our parents. It's not fair. When you marry, you leave father and mother to be with your husband or wife, and they are your responsibility before your own parents." Sally says she has talked to her children about her wishes. "I'm hoping that I can be functional until the end. But I'd rather be in a rest home than have my kids take care of me."

This is not because she enjoys the thought. "It's awfully hard for me to visit the rest homes. I see so many elderly people who are just sitting there vegetating, with no one to care. I don't think most of them have proper care."

Nonetheless, she is quite firm on the subject. "I dearly love my children, but I would go to a rest home before I would go to live with them."

Residential Care Homes and Nursing Homes

In many cases, as in Sally's, a shared home ultimately becomes impossible. The next step is a nursing home or other institution. People very rarely choose this option unless they have no other choice. Often, they do it from a sense of great desperation. What factors lead people to this?

- The primary caregiver becomes exhausted or sick, and there are no others available. This is often the case when the dependent elder becomes extremely senile, loses control of elimination, gets violent or hostile, or exhibits uninhibited sexual behavior (such as public masturbation). Sometimes, however, it happens when the elder is relatively alert and able, but due to health, job, emotional stability, or other reasons, the caregiver is simply not able to juggle these demanding duties. So it happened to Sally when her husband was disabled and she had to return to work.
- There is not enough money to care for the elder at home. As it stands today, Medicare and Medicaid will usually not pay for home care, even though it is often less expensive than nursing home care. Medicaid will, however, pick up the tab for a nursing home if a person is indigent. So a nursing home is often less expensive for the family (though the family must demonstrate that nursing home care is medically required).
- Caring for the elder is so disruptive to the home that others suffer. Children may feel neglected; a marriage may deteriorate.

Nursing Homes in Perspective

It is difficult to keep nursing homes in perspective since, at any given time, only 5 percent of people over 65 inhabit them. Yet they loom very large in any discussion of old age. This is partly because they are visible and public. We do not see the millions of homebound, unless we happen to be related to them. Anyone who visits a friend or family member in a nursing home, however, is made aware of the large population of others in a like situation. The sheer numbers, and the institutional sterility, often seem oppressive.

More oppressive can be the condition of those being cared for. Not all—many show life, intelligence and joy. But many others only nod, shuffle, moan or mutter—if that. Sometimes even the best nursing home seems like a living hell.

Is there any way to change this picture? Not that anyone has yet imagined. All proposals for nursing home reform are marginal. They would, arguably, make a difference, but they would not change the kind of people who need nursing home care.

About one out of four people die within their first year of entering a nursing home; half die within three years. Some of these deaths are probably due to the psychological environment of the home; many people witness elders "giving up" and, though the effect probably can't be precisely measured, too many people see it for us to dismiss it. Still, we must be realistic about the physical condition people are in before they enter a nursing home. People die in emergency rooms, too, but that doesn't mean the emergency room caused their death. Many people enter emergency rooms—and nursing homes—already sick enough to die.

Those who adjust best to nursing homes are vigorous, energetic people who make up their minds to thrive there— and believe it or not, some people do just that. If an aging person enters a nursing home already sick and depleted, however, he or she may have no reserve energy to face the adjustment. People naturally put off entering a nursing home until they have, literally, exhausted every other possibility. It's at least arguable that they would have done better (and lived longer) had they made that hard choice sooner.

There are two other reasons for considering a nursing home before you absolutely have to. One is the fact that nursing homes tend to favor admitting people who don't require constant care. Such patients, since they put less of a burden on the staff, are good for the nursing home. (It's also easier to get into the best homes if you have medical insurance that covers nursing home care. Some don't take Medicaid at all.)

The other reason has to do with the mindset of the children. The director of services on aging for the Federation of Protestant Welfare Agencies in New York is quoted this way by Otten and Shelley: "The decision to seek admission for a parent to an institution is not lightly taken in most families. But, once done, families begin to move like lightning because the whole procedure is so painful for them." They make up their minds in a flurry, sometimes in as little as 24 hours—too little time to make a careful choice. If circumstances suggest that sooner or later a nursing home will be necessary, then it's good to work through the decision before you're forced to.

Choosing a Nursing Home

How do you recognize a good nursing home? No *Consumer's Report* rates them, so families have to make the best choice possible with limited information. It's an important decision, since there are big differences between them, and few people in the Fifth Day can just up and move if the place doesn't work out.

Start by asking advice. Doctors, especially internists or family practitioners, see plenty of nursing homes. They may be reluctant to rate institutions, but probably will if you ask point-blank. Pastors who call on the elderly are another good source of information and may be more attuned to the spiritual and social environment, which is just as important as the quality of medical care.

When you have a short list of possibilities, it's time to use the phone. Ask about the level of care offered (your doctor will tell you what's appropriate); whether they are currently accepting new residents or have a waiting list; requirements (financial or medical) for new residents; and finally, if you're still interested, when you can come to visit and meet the director.

Most people suggest making at least two visits. You want to feel the ambience of the place, and meet some of the staff. You want to get a sense of whether or not this can be "home."

On your first visit, you should meet the director, take a tour, and get an answer to some basic questions. On your second visit, preferably at a different time of day, you should come unannounced and see what you find.

My mother says that she would want a nursing home with good Christian services and Bible studies. A friend of hers, who loves to talk politics, felt extremely enthusiastic about a home in downtown Newark where she had plenty of stimulating conversation. She moved there after rejecting a beautiful "Grandma Moses" home a long drive from all her friends.

Many books offer lists of questions and concerns that should be raised, but the most important issue is probably the quality of staff and administration. Good people can make almost any facility work. Still, that quality is hard to judge on a visit. Here, gleaned from a number of sources, is a short list of issues to consider:

1. What is the philosophy of the nursing home?
2. Who owns it? Is it for profit or not?
3. What kind of contract would be signed? Ask to see one. Note the charges for "extras," which can vary tremendously.
4. What is the resident-staff ratio?
5. What staff members are available, and on what shifts? Social workers, physical therapists, activity directors: what hours do they work, and what facilities do they have to use?
6. Is there a chaplain? What religious activities are sponsored? What other programs and activities are sponsored? (It may be good to visit one of these.)
7. Note the administrator's presence, availability, and manner with patients.
8. Observe the condition of the patients. Are they dressed? Out of bed? In a TV coma? Do they seem clean?
9. Visit the kitchen. Do they have a nutritionist? Who prepares the menus? Ask to see one. Eat a meal.
10. Talk to some of the staff, including orderlies (who do much of the daily routine).
11. If you see something you don't like, *ask about it.* It's helpful to find out how the staff responds to questions and complaints *before* you're making them about treatment for a member of your own family (or for yourself).

Paying the Cost of Nursing Homes

A word about finances: nursing homes are expensive. Figure, very roughly speaking, on $15,000 to $35,000 per year. It's cheaper to send someone to college.

People argue that home care is less expensive. That depends. If you have to hire someone every day (including weekends and holidays) for an eight-hour shift, it may well be more expensive. And, remember another important factor: Medicaid, at this point, will pay for nursing homes, but not for most home care expenses.

Medicaid varies from state to state, and since their formula is constantly changing, it's hard to give an exact picture of how it applies. Again: Medicare is for everybody, but Medicaid is only for people who have almost no money left. (The children's finances are not considered, only those of the elder concerned.) Medicare only covers a limited time in a nursing home—150 days per year, for sickness, not custodial care. Medicaid will generally pay *all* the bills at an inexpensive nursing home.

Will Medicare or Medicaid soon be expanded to cover home care? Right now that seems unlikely. The only way for the government to make good judgments about who truly needs such help would be to send a flood of social workers to pry into people's personal affairs. The government is understandably wary of this.

As is, about $20 billion is paid for nursing home care each year in America; half of this, by the government. A lot of people grouse that you only get government help after you've spent all your life savings, but what are life savings for, if not to pay for your old age? Why should others pay those bills in order for an elder to pass on a nest egg to the next generation? As the system works today, a senior can maintain possession of his house (if it's paid for), his car, and a small bank account. That's so that if he recovers, he's not stuck in the nursing home. In many states, these assets must go to the state to reimburse Medicaid costs after the senior dies.

Very often, people enter the nursing home with money in the bank and pay the bills themselves until they run out of money. It can happen fast, at $20,000 a year. Then the government takes over payments.

Incidentally, very few children choose to pay rather than letting the government do so. Between 1 and 2 percent of nursing home bills are paid by relatives. Sometimes a parent will be unwilling to spend his own money to enter a nursing home, simply because he wants to preserve an inheritance to pass on. He may expect his children to pay the bills. This strategy should be resisted firmly. Most families would be bankrupted in no time!

After Ben's second stroke, his children were faced with a difficult decision. The doctor had said he needed full-time care, and they could not see how to provide it at his home or theirs. They finally decided that Ben would have to enter a nursing home, though they knew how hard it would be for him to give up his independence. They cleaned out his apartment and divided his belongings; Ben took only a favorite chair and a television set with him.

Because of his stroke, Ben's memory was fuzzy. One night he got into bed with a woman, and when the nurse came and led him back to his own room, he said, "Well, I usually sleep with my wife."

He had lost interest in reading and in sports, his life-long passion. He seemed depressed, and though he could walk and was able to feed himself he showed no interest in interacting with others. He usually sat with the television on, paying scant attention to the daily visits made by his son or daughter-in-law.

One summer day, with the temperature at 107, Ben disappeared. The nurses said he had been talking all morning about going home. His son called the police, then drove around the area looking for him. Ben was found that evening, six hours after his disappearance, sitting on a woman's front lawn, several miles from the convalescent hospital. Ben had been unable to tell her who he was or where he was from, but she had read his wristband and called for help.

The nursing home thought that, for his own safety, Ben ought to be in a locked facility. Ben's son begged them to let Ben stay, and they finally relented, but they tied him into his chair while they were feeding the other patients.

One night he escaped in his wheelchair, which they found outside, abandoned. This time Ben was out all night while they frantically hunted for him. Ben had crossed a field and come to a vacant garage, where a trained Doberman stood guard. The dog, apparently sensing that Ben was no threat, let him in to sleep for the night. The next morning Ben tapped on the window of the house. The woman who lived there ran out the front door and across the street to call the police. When they arrived, the Doberman would not let them near Ben. Finally the woman called her dog off, and the police took Ben back to the nursing home. He said he was trying to get back to his apartment. He had scratches on his face; he evidently had fallen and lost his glasses.

After his second escape, he was put into a locked facility. A little lady named Emma, who thought Ben was her husband, attached herself to him. Usually when the family visited Ben, it was hard to get away from Emma, whom Ben often called "that pest." (He also occasionally called her his wife.) Most of the people who lived in the locked facility were quite senile; one man wore a huge hat and marched around and around the square formed by hallways; a woman was constantly scolding another in a wild, nightmarish voice.

Ben's son and daughter-in-law still visited often, though not daily as before. The doctor encouraged them to relax a bit, and since Ben couldn't remember whether they had just been there or not, the frequency of their visits didn't seem critical. Sometimes they took him home with them, but it was harder to bring him back. An attendant would lock the door behind them, and they could look back at Ben, staring at them through the window.

Sometimes Ben was nearly himself. Shortly before his death, Ben's daughter came to visit. He knew her and her husband immediately, and they all went out to the courtyard to avoid Emma. They visited for several hours.

Ben asked about his grandchildren. He took them on a tour of the facilities and seemed to take pride in where he lived. It was a prized day, one to remember: a gift from God. The next day, a Sunday, Ben's son brought him home, but Ben was confused and slept most of the time.

Not many weeks afterwards, Ben had a bad stroke, went into a coma and never regained consciousness. His daughter, who had been on the way to take her own daughter to college, said she felt a strange confusion of grief afterwards. It took her weeks to realize that though her father was permanently gone, her daughter was not; she would see her daughter again.

Happiness in a Nursing Home

When someone like Ben enters a nursing home, he loses a great deal of himself. Nobody asks or cares much about how he spent his previous years. His hobbies or interests no longer matter. Even if he has a lot of money in the bank, he can't do much with it. Of his possessions, he can keep only those that fit into his room. He completely lacks prestige or status. Virtually the only thing he cannot lose is his history with his family. He also cannot lose the love of God: "Neither death nor life, neither angels nor demons, neither the present nor the future, nor any powers, neither height nor depth, nor anything else in all creation, will be able to separate us from the love of God that is in Christ Jesus our Lord" (Rom. 8:38–39).

For most, then, family and faith remain the most important things in their world. Even so, they may doubt them both. In fact, since so much of their self-identity is devastated, nursing home residents often become quite anxious or depressed. They may feel that nobody loves or remembers them—including God. Once, when their lives were full of other things, a monthly visit from a child was plenty; now once a day doesn't seem often enough. Similarly with God's love, as they look daily for evidences of his love, they may feel that he is hiding from them.

According to one survey, as many as 40 percent of nursing home residents have "excess disability." That is, they act worse than their disabilities should merit. Though they could still walk, they quit walking. Though they could still talk, they quit talking. We are hardly in a position to judge such people. We do not know even a fraction of the struggles they endure. But we can at least observe that not everyone sinks into despair.

Some rise above their disabilities and losses. Elizabeth Wrightman, for years a nursing home activities director, told me, "I learned how to live life as an adult through watching old people in the nursing home." She observed some people whose lives collapsed in the face of adversity. There were others whose faith and hope in God enabled them to flourish spiritually. "If heaven and hell start here on earth," she says, "the paths begin to diverge in the nursing home."

Key Attitudes

My father has visited hundreds of nursing home residents over the years of his ministry, and he emphasizes that their situation is not necessarily grim. "More than half the time the particular person I visited was having a good day. Some had a great experience in very poor places. The majority were happy."

He isolates four factors that made the difference in their outlook. First, they accepted *relative* contentment. They were mature enough to have learned that everything doesn't have to be perfect. "If you have to be happy every day, all the time, you will be miserable," he says.

Second, they had a *relative* acceptance of their dependency while fighting back in symbolic ways (for instance, insisting on certain ways their meal should be served). A balance between independence and dependence is desirable. Too much resistance to dependence makes a person unhappy, but so does total dependence.

Third, "If they saw themselves as instruments to help and serve those around them, they were likely to be happy."

Finally, faith in God, for most, really made a difference.

My father told me about a woman he knew in a Kansas nursing home. She had become discouraged and depressed because she couldn't do all she used to do for others. "What is it that you used to do?" he asked her. "I made them pies sometimes," she said. "And I would smile and cheer them up."

"Well, you can still smile," he told her. But she had a hard time thinking that there was anything valuable about a smile without a pie to accompany it.

Then one day my father visited her along with my grandfather, who was a resident in the same nursing home. My grandfather could not, then, say an intelligible word. But he still had charisma, and people respected him. He greeted the woman, who seemed unusually discouraged, and then said, as clear as a bell, "You always have the nicest smile." After that no more intelligible words came out of him. But from this small miracle the woman seemed to draw encouragement and stopped struggling with a sense of purposelessness. She began to smile.

I met a man named Calvin in a nursing home where I visited regularly. Calvin had been a gardener, and as much as any man I have known, he loved growing things. However, a heart condition had forced Calvin to give up digging in the garden. He had a row of potted geraniums in his window, but he scorned them as insignificant. Unfortunately, Calvin had never learned to take an interest in other human beings. He had lost track of his children years before and had no time for other residents. Even though he was mentally alert and generally in good health, he was very unhappy.

Another man, Robert, lived down the hall from Calvin. Robert was in worse shape physically. His hands shook, and he walked haltingly. However, Robert took an interest in people. He was proud of his family and displayed their pictures in his room. He talked with other residents. There was a world of difference between Robert and Calvin—a world of difference that had been developed over a lifetime. The difference was that Robert cared about people, and Calvin cared about plants. I have a great deal of admiration for those who live close to the earth. But at 80, the earth is no substitute for personal relationships.

The best thing families can do for nursing home residents is to kindle their interest in people. And the people they will most likely be interested in, and to whom they may offer the most, are their own family members. Cultivating family relationships is important, not merely in itself, but because it strengthens the elder's sense of his or her own significance.

Visiting in the Fifth Day

Regular visits are probably the most important thing you, as a child of the nursing home resident, can offer. They need not, in fact they usually should not, be long. It's best if they are on a schedule, so that they can be enjoyed in anticipation as well as in execution.

If an elder can no longer converse, there are other things

to do. Touch. Hug. Give a back rub. Kiss. Sing a song. Bring a gift—a flower, a photo, a picture, a magazine. Bring a child along. Bring a pet. Really listen, and try to understand, even if it's not easy. The concern communicates, even when the words do not.

If your older friend or relative sometimes forgets that you've been there, write a note on the spot giving thanks for the visit, and noting the day and the time. That provides a tangible reminder of the visit. If you're far away, or even if you're not, letters and cards are always valuable. They are enjoyed a dozen times over. They're also a status symbol in the nursing home—proof that somebody cares.

Pictures are a great aid to conversation, allowing you to summon up the presence of many others, past and present. John Gillies tells how he made a photo album, with captions, of his mother's life. It allowed others (nurses' aides, for instance) to catch a glimpse of the kind of woman she was, and how she had lived her life. And it made his mother aware of the world outside the nursing home—especially the world of family who loved her. Often when he visited her, after her memory was largely gone, they thumbed through the album together.

Invest time in getting to know the staff. They hear a lot of complaining, but little thanks and good cheer. The staff will do a better job if they are encouraged and recognized, and they'll surely take more interest in your parent or loved one if they get to know you. Incidentally, don't be too quick to believe elders' complaints. Nursing home residents don't always have an objective grasp of their circumstances. Items are stolen occasionally, but they can also be misplaced or given away and then forgotten. Sometimes aides are slow to answer buzzers, but their record may be better than it is perceived to be. Residents also complain that their relatives never visit them—and that's not always accurate, either.

If you get to know the staff, you can take up complaints without always being "the complainer."

Try to think creatively of how to encourage your loved one to serve others. Service may be a question of smiling— nothing more. In most nursing homes, smiles are not common currency, and they mean a lot. Many residents will be capable of more: of sharing their memories on cassette, of communicating love to their grandchildren, of communicating love to *foster* grandchildren. Some programs connect elders to service in children's daycare centers.

When elders help others, they themselves are helped. If you are living for your own pleasure past 80, you are bound to get discouraged. But if you are living for others, there is always something to do.

At the age of 76, Genevieve had lived in nursing homes for seven years. Her nursing home years had been discouraging: she had been highly medicated and had spent all of her time in bed. When not heavily sedated, she had severe tremors and was greatly agitated. It appeared that life in the usual sense was over for Genevieve. Communication with others could not readily take place because she was either hyperventilating and terrified, or nearly asleep from her drug therapy.

Fortunately, a change of nursing homes availed Genevieve of a change of personnel and medicine. She began to respond. She was now in an environment where she was expected to be up and dressed daily, out of her room if possible, and attending group activities. This happy combination provided just what Genevieve needed. Very slowly she began to recover her confidence.

She began to get around in her wheelchair and meet other residents. In response to invitations from a staff member, Genevieve attempted once or twice to go out to church. Her faith, which had lain dormant during her severe illness, began to grow strong again. Genevieve, in fact, was transformed. She was able to share her faith in a quiet and very mature way. Years of suffering and hopelessness had not permanently discouraged her.

Now Genevieve could be found in the lobby daily, talking with other residents and counseling with them. She understood their fears of illness and of becoming confused. She, who had once been so agitated and desperate, was now calm and attentive to others. She did not avoid people who repeated themselves. She appeared to have infinite patience for each anxious newcomer.

Genevieve became the mail lady. In her wheelchair she would deliver the mail to the rooms of the residents. The mail lady died very unexpectedly, and many people found it painful to say good-bye. Genevieve had reached out to others to heal and to care as soon as Christ had given her the strength to do so.

> (from an unpublished paper by
> Elizabeth Wrightman)

Strengthening Faith

Not everybody can match Genevieve. In fact, not even Genevieve could match Genevieve so long as she was drugged and hysterical. But she reminds us that there are real triumphs in nursing homes. Some people, though they seem to have nothing to offer, manage to convey faith and cheer and encouragement to others.

It's important for families to creatively foster faith in God. Strangely enough, faith often gets sidelined for older people, as though they had outgrown their need for it, or as though, conversely, they were "naturally" religious and needed no encouragement.

Yet many older people will be thinking about their faith in God, wondering whether it will survive the losses of the Fifth Day. As they approach death they may wonder, "Will I still believe?"

Faith is not automatic at any stage of life. Some people do lose faith as they grow older, and some gain. The majority, though, seem to hold on to the same beliefs that have sustained them throughout life. These apply their faith to new struggles, and learn new lessons. Sometimes a very small seed of faith, planted during childhood but neglected since then, takes root and grows very strong.

People at any age gain a great deal of support from living in a community with other believers, and from the visible symbols of faith—gathering to worship on Sunday morning, particularly. When people can no longer get out for church, they lose these supports. They lose touch with believers, and seldom if ever worship in a congregation. Without any visible structure, their faith can seem unreal and irrelevant to their present circumstances.

Yet faith remains real and relevant, if it is true at all. Families can encourage nursing home residents to maintain or grow in their faith by reading or studying Scripture with them; by praying with or for them; by talking about heaven; by sharing news of the church; by playing cassettes of hymns, or singing them; by bringing cassettes of church services; by providing reading materials; by making sure elders know when TV church services will be broadcast, and on what channel, and by helping them select a TV service they will enjoy and benefit from.

Many nursing homes have their roots in a particular church, and even those that don't are often aware of the "spiritual needs" of residents. Many offer regular services sponsored by local churches; some have chaplaincy services available. But if the staff isn't alert to your parent's interest, they may not invite him or her to join in such services. Many nursing homes make only casual attempts to encourage attendance by residents. You can ask the nursing home administration what programs are offered, and then talk directly to the program leaders, asking them to be sure to include your parent. You may want to participate yourself as a sure way of knowing what's happening. If your parent's room is changed—as frequently happens, usually without any notice to others—make sure that these leaders know the new room number.

I believe many families grow slightly embarrassed about their faith when they enter a nursing home; their good news seems irrelevant to the suffering and loss they see about them. This attitude is related to a modern truism, that "you can't preach to a starving man." It's not true. You cannot preach to a starving man while withholding food from him. But starving men are often quite interested in eternity. So are nursing home residents. There's really nothing more important than the kind of faith they have as they approach death, and where that orientation will take them after death.

Herb grew plums. For 37 years he had taught machine shop at the local junior college, but he was retired from that. The plum ranch now kept him fully occupied. Herb was a mechanical whiz, and something of a perfectionist. In the last few years, though, he had seemed to take less interest in keeping up the ranch. He seemed listless. His wife Elita had noticed, but just chalked it up to old age. After all, Herb was 80.

He went into town one day to get a license for spraying from the Agriculture Commission. He'd done it dozens of times before. This time he came home sobbing. He told Elita that he couldn't find the place.

Herb's wife took him to a doctor who asked questions like, "Who's the President of the United States?" Herb didn't know. The doctor told Elita that Herb had Alzheimer's disease. "It's irreversible," he said.

"Those are hard words," Elita says. The shock was terrible for her. She thought it was less so for Herb. His tears, she thought, came from temporary frustration, not the realization that he was losing his memory. He didn't even seem to be aware of his condition. For herself, though, she says, "They say it's the heartbreak disease, and it is."

Eventually, Herb not only forgot where the Agriculture Commission was, he couldn't remember how to put gas in the car. He slept more and more, and his balance got worse. Twice he fell in the bathroom. Once he took off toward the highway, and Elita feared for his life. Fortunately she was able to stop him.

He didn't like to be left alone. Not long after his diagnosis, Elita and their daughter Marilyn came in from the garden and found him pacing nervously. "I thought you fellas were *never* going to get back," he said. After that, they left him notes whenever they left the house. But Elita was away as little as possible. Once a month she went to a meeting, and had a neighbor stay with Herb. She left a note even so, and the neighbor told her Herb picked it up and read it at least twenty times.

Herb began to have trouble separating fact from fiction. They stopped watching TV because the shows alarmed him so. At night he was restless. Once he thrashed around so violently in a nightmare he gave Elita a black eye. A friend advised her to sleep somewhere else. But Elita said, "He's my husband and I've slept with him for sixty years."

Sometimes, when neighbors came over, Herb would perk up. Once a friend sat down by Herb and gave him a kiss. He said to her, "That was nice, but I don't know who you are."

They sold the ranch—it was hard for Herb to sign the papers—but continued to live there. Their only living daughter Marilyn had been going through a divorce, so there was heartache all around. She came and stayed for three months; then a sister came to stay. The sister grew worried about Elita. She wrote a letter to the doctor, suggesting that the load was too much and that Herb should be in a convalescent hospital. None of the nursing homes nearby had space, however.

Eventually they found a nursing home in the town

where Marilyn lived, several hours' drive away. They were very anxious about how Herb would accept the move. Driving over in the car, he kept fiddling nervously with all the knobs and handles; once he almost opened the door, but responded to Marilyn's frantic cries. When they got to the nursing home, the nurses handled him beautifully. He went in peacefully. Elita moved in with her daughter.

Herb didn't walk during the eighteen months he lived in the nursing home. They sat with him often, Marilyn playing cards or doing needlepoint; Elita, feeding him. During the last three months of his life, he didn't recognize Marilyn. Once, when she told him, "I'm your daughter," he broke into a big smile and said, "Is that right?" His last words to his wife, one week before he died from a kidney infection, were, "Do I know you?"

Alzheimer's Disease and Senile Dementia

Alzheimer's disease has undoubtedly been with us for as long as people have grown old, but was practically unknown until recently. Doctors thought that senile dementia (commonly called "senility") was a result of decreased blood supply to the brain, and that it was just part of getting old. Now we know that the majority of cases of senile dementia are caused by Alzheimer's, a specific disease which attacks the brain and gradually causes it to stop functioning. It can affect young people, though it is far more common among the elderly.

The disease tends to run its course in an average of seven years, though in slow-moving cases the torment can last much longer. First the memory goes, gradually slipping away. The victim loses his or her ability to work, forgetting names, places, routines that are essential. Eventually the routines of daily living—tying shoes, bathing, brushing teeth—are lost to memory. Sometimes the personality is altered dramatically, so that a gentle grandparent becomes violent, for instance. Finally the brain even "forgets" basic body functions, and the Alzheimer's victim curls into a fetal position and dies.

With increased awareness and longer lives, more cases are reported—so many that Alzheimer's was called "the disease of the century" before AIDS replaced it. The cover story in a 1984 issue of *Newsweek* reported that about 7 percent of Americans over 65 are severely disabled by the disease, with women three times as likely to have it as men. The longer people live, however, the greater are their chances of developing symptoms. (The risk levels are 4–5 percent for ages 65–74; 10–15 percent for ages 75–84; and 20 percent for ages 85 and up.) Like cancer, Alzheimer's disease has become an epidemic largely because people are living longer.

Increased awareness means that Alzheimer's is no longer treated with a shrug of the shoulders. Medical researchers are working hard for a cure, and as they understand the disease better, their hope expands. While at this point no cure exists, doctors and other caring professionals are now far more aware of the progressive nature of the disease, and the way it can devastate both patient and family. They can't do away with the devastation, but they can help cushion the shocks.

The negative side of increased awareness is that older people are terrified by Alzheimer's. "Losing your mind" ranks as one of their outstanding fears, and all the publicity about Alzheimer's has served only to heighten panic. Very, very often seniors are anxiously monitoring the loss of their short-term memory. When they forget names or lose their keys, they fear that it is the first sign.

Often this anxiety will be expressed in a halfhearted joke, or an aside. Relatives and friends should be alert for such concerns. There is evidence that short-term memory normally declines in old age, but this memory loss ordinarily has nothing to do with Alzheimer's. At least you can reassure an elder that her forgetfulness seems normal to you.

Unfortunately, you can't be much more definite. There is no test to establish *positively* whether a person has Alzheimer's. The disease is diagnosed by screening out other possibilities. (This is called a "diagnosis of exclusion.") If doctors can't find anything else wrong with you, they call it Alzheimer's. So elders who forget names or addresses will undoubtedly keep on worrying.

They have a genuine reason to worry when memory loss interferes with their ability to function. Then it is crucial that they see a doctor experienced in the diagnosis and treatment of Alzheimer's. There are many causes of dementia other than Alzheimer's, and some of them are reversible. It's extremely important that the diagnosis be correct, and this requires considerable skill.

The second greatest cause of mental confusion is a stroke or a series of strokes. While strokes, which damage the brain, cannot be reversed, with good rehabilitation other parts of the brain can sometimes be retrained to take over the functions that were lost. Strokes need not lead to gradual degeneration: with proper medication, there may be no recurrences.

Other causes of senile dementia may be completely reversible. Since the body chemistry of older people changes dramatically, they sometimes react with mental confusion to a combination of drugs, for instance. Malnutrition can have the same effect. Even stress or grief or an unfamiliar setting (hospital rather than home) can lead to extended senile episodes. Not every doctor is trained to distinguish these from Alzheimer's or stroke damage; unfortunately, some doctors still dismiss patients as merely "getting old."

But "getting old" is not what makes people sick; it merely makes them vulnerable. A specific medical condition makes them sick. If you know what it is, you can sometimes do something about it.

Talking to the Mentally Confused

The care of those who are mentally confused, particularly the care of Alzheimer's victims, is a subject of its own. Here I would like to restrict my attention to the question of friendship and spiritual encouragement, as it will usually be expressed in visiting.

Perhaps the most persistent difficulty for the visitor is believing that there really is any such thing as friendship and spiritual encouragement. We tend to think, in a rationalistic sort of way, that relationships and spiritual life last only as long as our rational faculties do. It is discouraging to continue faithfully with a loved one who cannot, for instance, remember who you are. But those who work regularly with such people believe that continuing your relationship has real, substantial value. They point out that a confused person may not know her husband, but she still recognizes a smile, a warm embrace, a gift wrapped up in ribbons. A person whose short-term memory is gone may be unable to articulate the gospel, but he still can be moved by the melody of "Amazing Grace," and its rhythm and mood may communicate its theme—the grace of God—directly to his soul.

Do we really know enough about spiritual growth to be able to measure it? Might there be development of love and faith in a blasted mind that we are incapable of seeing, but that matters to God a great deal? Do we know what sorts of tests and temptations a confused person suffers? I do not think we know much more about spiritual life during this period than we know about the spiritual life of a baby. But in both cases we know that they are human beings who deserve, merely by being alive, our concern and love.

Arthur Becker, with many years of pastoral counseling in such situations, commends three strategies from Dr. Albert Meiburg. They are (1) to help focus the person's attention on the visit; (2) to help the person stay in touch with reality; and (3) to find meaning in the person's experiences and expressions.

First, to focus attention on the visit, try to remove distractions. Almost all people, no matter how confused, are lucid some of the time. You want to increase the chances of that possibility. The privacy of a quiet room is likely to be better than a crowded hallway. Tactfully see that hearing aids are on and that glasses are worn. Pay attention to the way you speak: loudly, distinctly, slowly. Touch often helps to focus attention—holding hands while you talk, for instance. In any case, the touch communicates something words cannot.

Make sure you address the person you've come to visit. It's easier to talk to a nurse, and that's exactly what some visitors do. Make an effort to break through to real communication. Don't say "I understand" if you don't. Your fiction will soon become obvious, and communication will grind hopelessly to a halt. It's better to work hard for partial communication than to pretend that conversation is proceeding when, in fact, it isn't. For some people, communication will be better if you use a large pad of paper and a felt marker, and write out what you want to say. You can also leave a message to remind your loved one of the visit. It doesn't have to be "I love you" every time. It could be a joke, or even a picture.

Second, try to help your loved one focus on reality. In some nursing homes this is called "reality therapy." For instance, a patient will be carefully told each day where he is, what the day is, how the weather looks outside. It helps to know exactly what therapy is being done, and to try to reinforce it. In any case, address the person you're visiting by name, and tell him your own name. (Don't ask, "Do you know who I am?" If he's in any doubt, his anxiety will be increased.) Salt your conversation with news of the outside world. You'll have to try to judge for yourself how much news is practical; knowing who is president is all some can handle, while others will appreciate hearing about family, church, neighborhood, public affairs. You can also refer carefully to the time you last visited, and tell specifically when you plan to come next.

What about delusions the elder raises? Suppose, for instance, that you told your mother that you had missed seeing her for the last two days because you had been on a trip to St. Louis, and she rejoined that she had been on a trip to Paris. What do you say? It doesn't usually help to argue that she's never been to Paris, nor is it helpful to encourage her. ("How were things in Paris?") But what should you say?

That question brings us to the third strategy: to try to find meaning in the person's experiences and expressions. This usually requires putting together a symbolic puzzle.

Very often, for mentally confused people

- Feelings replace logic.
- They express themselves in concrete symbols.
- They see things in black and white. Somebody either loves them or hates them, for instance.
- Time is all jumbled up, so that what happened thirty years ago may be treated as present reality.

The result is that what a visitor hears sounds quite bizarre. But, warns Meiburg, "Although the communications of a confused person may be logically incongruous, on a feeling level there is a basis for reality."

The hard part is interpreting what that reality is. Take, for example, the mother who "took a trip to Paris." The question you want to ask yourself is, "What does it mean for her to take a trip to Paris?" Perhaps Paris is your mother's favorite city; then you might try responding, "You've been very happy, then?" Or if your mother last visited Paris on her honeymoon fifty years ago, you might say, "Have you been thinking about Dad?" Or perhaps she is merely saying to you, "I'm an important person, too."

There is no use pretending that the interpretation of these statements is easy. Some people believe that senile fantasies are a means for elders to work out deep issues, spiritual and psychological. You may never be quite sure you have understood what was going on. But sometimes, as though by magic, you will "connect." And sometimes you as a visitor will catch a glimpse of the difficulties your parent or friend struggles with, and this will enable you to be more compassionate in your care and in your prayers. Even the attempt to understand is valuable. It tells an aging person that he is loved, that someone takes him seriously, that someone is listening.

DAY 6

MEMO TO MY FATHER:

SOMETIME YEARS BACK—I THINK I WAS IN college, with the Vietnam draft hanging over my head—I spoke to you about my dread of death. I had only just discovered it in myself—only just then allowed myself to look down that dark channel. It gave me the frenzies.

I thought your response a little strange. You did not try to tell me that my fears were unnecessary, since death was a passageway to the resurrection. You merely said, "It won't be so frightening when you get older."

I have found this true. I still fear death, but not nearly so much as I did. I expect to grow even less afraid. For as I have talked to people older than myself and asked them about death, I have often found them as much curious as frightened.

We do grow accustomed to it, and yet never quite. A friend of mine put it this way at 93: "I don't feel afraid of death. Dread, maybe."

Most probably, I will watch you face it before I take my turn.

I am still afraid to see you go—afraid for you, and afraid for myself. I do not want to die, and I do not want you to die, though we must. Why the fear? Is death not the most natural thing in the world? I do not believe that it is.

The Sixth Day: Saying Good-bye

LINDA FIRST LEARNED THAT SOMETHING WAS wrong when her mother called to say that they wouldn't be making a weekend visit. She was vague. "Daddy's not up to it." "Is he sick?" Linda asked. Her mother said no. After hanging up, Linda broke into tears. She felt something was very wrong.

Linda learned that her father had become disoriented, having trouble with his balance and his memory. He saw a doctor the following Monday. By Wednesday they had the test results. Don had a brain tumor.

Linda and her sister were with their mother for the surgery. They prayed with Don beforehand, and Linda shared a verse with him: "'You will not have to fight this battle. Take up your positions; stand firm and see the deliverance the LORD will give you. . . . Do not be afraid; do not be discouraged. Go out to face them tomorrow, and the LORD will be with you'" (2 Chron. 20:17).

The surgery lasted for thirteen hours. During that entire period, no one came out to report on Don's progress. The three women prayed and sang hymns. At one o'clock in the morning the surgeon came to explain that they had found a huge tumor and removed 90 percent of it, but had been forced to leave the remaining 10 percent.

Linda watched her mother's face as the doctor told her the news. Linda had never seen such anguish and heartache. Nevertheless, her mother kept her composure and asked the doctor all the right questions. After he had gone, she turned to her daughters and said, "What are we going to tell Daddy?"

They went home, too full of grief to sleep. That night they stayed together in the same room.

The next few days were spent in the hospital. Don didn't ask about the surgery, and they didn't volunteer any information. Perhaps he knew from their faces. A few days after the surgery, however, they received very good news. Laboratory tests had established that the tumor was benign and slow-growing. They felt extremely thankful, and went to the chapel to praise God. Don received radiation treatments. His prognosis looked positive.

About a year later, however, problems with Don's hearing led the doctors to discover tiny tumors on each ear nerve. Again he had surgery. One tumor was removed, since hearing in that ear was already destroyed. The doctors left the remaining tumor, otherwise Don would have lost all hearing. He suffered some facial paralysis as a result of the surgery. Afterwards he gave up driving. His wife Sally began to make many of the family decisions.

At the end of the first year following surgery, Don seemed much improved. Linda and her husband Bill went on a trip, and her parents came to watch their three kids. They had planned to stay on for a few days after Linda and Bill returned. But their plans changed; Sally said they would have to go home immediately. Don had been disoriented during the week. He hadn't been able to remember where Linda and Bill had gone.

The doctors scheduled Don for exploratory surgery. Unfortunately, Linda and her family all had come down with chicken pox, and were too contagious to leave home. She stayed at home, praying. After the surgery her sister called with the news. Don's brain cells had begun to die—a rare side effect of radiation.

All they could do was cry. Linda said to her sister, over and over, "Poor Mom, poor Daddy, poor Mom, poor Daddy." The next day her contagious phase had ended, and she went to join her mother, taking her year-old baby and leaving the two older children with her husband and with friends.

For the next four months Linda lived between her home and her mother's home. The hour-and-a-half drive gave her a chance to shift her thoughts from one place to another.

Her father needed help eating now, even swallowing. After he left the hospital, he entered a convalescent home. They talked to him, but were never very sure how much he understood. Once he addressed Linda by name when she walked in. Once he said, "Bye-bye."

In the last two months of his life, he fell completely silent. They kept talking, but never knew whether he understood. They did not know whether he would live another day, or another year. Linda drew great strength from her faith in God. "I couldn't face the day without opening my Bible and reading a psalm to get the strength to go ahead." She prayed for a miracle. Then in the last month, she prayed for the Lord to take him.

They had told the doctor not to take measures to extend

Don's life. The night of his death they left to go home and sleep. Linda said to him, "Good night, Daddy. I love you. I'll see you in the morning."

The next morning, a call came. He had died in the night. Linda felt some anger that the staff hadn't called them at the time. But her mother said she had prayed that Linda and her sister wouldn't have to go through a terrible death-bed scene. She thought God had been merciful to them.

Indeed, that sense of mercy remained with them all. They had had time to prepare to lose him, to say good-bye. "It was the hardest thing I've ever been through," Linda says, "and yet, I don't think I've ever been as close to the Lord before or since."

Fear of Death

Elders may well skip the losses and dependency of the Third, Fourth and Fifth Days of the week. They will not skip the Sixth Day. Here everyone comes together.

Younger people seem to think that the elderly are consumed by the fear of death. But old people usually claim it is not so. They rarely express a strong fear of death; they do often fear the process of dying. They would like to get out of life without much pain. They would rather not drag it out, either. They don't want to act pitiful or ridiculous. But they cannot see any way to guarantee a calm and dignified death.

Death itself—the fact of leaving this life—seems less fearful when many of your friends have died. "I have as many friends on the other side as I do here," my 93-year-old friend told me. She can remember her father saying the same when he was nearing death.

Pat Parker, who visits the elderly for her church, writes that many shut-ins tell her they spend time every day talking to significant others who have died. One woman in her nineties said, "I talk to Clarissa [her cousin and companion who died a year before] every night; I tell her what's happened that day; do you think that's silly?" No, it certainly is not silly. Lonely, yes. Futile, perhaps. Yet it demonstrates the persistent human belief that the dead are not really dead, only removed from our sight. This belief may grow stronger as one ages, and the fear of death may grow less threatening.

Then, too, death may be less fearful when you have no plans to spoil. For those in their seventies or eighties, the slowing of life may have removed most earthly hopes, except those of seeing grandchildren or great-grandchildren grow. Ronald Blythe wrote in *View in Winter,* "You could compare old age with having worked hard all day and, by the time evening comes, finding that if you can manage to work just another hour you will have done all you could. The light isn't good enough to do any more, so you have to pack up. Finish."

Facing Imminent Death

There is a difference, though, between facing death from a distance, and facing it as an imminent prospect. Charles Moore, an older man who visits sick and dying people in the hospital, told me, "Most people are afraid. They say they're not afraid for the same reason people in a war say they're not afraid. They think, 'They're not going to call me.' Having visited so many dying people, I wonder how I will be. Just like I wonder if I had been in an army, would I have been afraid of going over that line in a charge."

Dying people don't find it easy to talk about their emotions, any more than most soldiers, preparing to attack, will sit in a foxhole and discuss their feelings. There's usually a desire for privacy. Arthur Becker writes, "During this time of dying the elder may prefer quiet companionship without much talking, or even solitude. Often there is a desire for the slowing down of personal relationships. Fewer visitors will be desired—perhaps none at all except for close family members." In some cases the dying person may literally "turn to the wall," escaping even his closest relatives. These may take this as a rejection; or they may feel that the dying person is deliberately being hostile. But people from time immemorial have turned their faces to the wall; it was considered, in other times, a perfectly normal way for a person to prepare to meet her Maker.

Horribly painful or difficult deaths are surprisingly rare, though some do occur. More often, people enter death quietly. According to one study cited by Morton Puner, about half of the elderly dying were in good contact with reality until they died; about 25 percent fluctuated between clarity and confusion, and 22 percent were in partial contact with reality. Only 3 percent were completely and consistently out of contact in their last days of life.

The Role of Friends and Relatives

The prospect of death often makes friends and relatives nervous. They don't know how to act or what to say. The first question is whether someone who is dying should be told he is dying. The modern answer tends to be, "Of course." Those who care for the dying, however, tend to be cautious. They mention their belief that most people, and particularly most elderly people, know full well that death is near. For their own reasons they may not wish to acknowledge this. We need not, they say, become too pushy about telling them they will die quite soon; the information ought not to be forced upon them.

Certainly, though, the truth should not be withheld from anyone who asks. People deserve to know what, if anything, is their business. If they want to discuss the medical and financial situation in detail, they should. (More often, they will simply want to know that others are taking care of it.) They may wish to discuss their life with God—to confess their sins, to pray, to be reassured by a pastor. There is nothing more natural than to wish to be prepared for death. The French historian Philippe Aries points out that what our time sometimes considers the ideal death—the one in your sleep, without warning—was in medieval times considered the worst possible way to die. It offered no time to prepare to meet God. Friends and family members ought to do what they can to encourage this preparation, rather than dodging the subject for fear of disturbing the dying person.

These days, spiritual concerns seem to be eclipsed by medical ones. Even with a durable power of attorney or living will making clear the dying person's wish not to prolong death, medical matters are rarely completely straightforward. Usually, the nearest relatives will become intimately involved with doctors. A helpful suggestion is that the family appoint one person—someone pleasant but not easily intimidated, who gets facts straight—to handle all discussions with the doctor. That way, the doctor doesn't have to repeat himself, and is less likely to resist lengthy question-and-answer sessions.

The decision not to continue the medical fight comes hard for many families; they feel they have no right to play God. But as Arthur Becker points out, we begin playing God long before then, when we give injections to children, or take medicine. We assume the right to some control over our destinies, even while knowing that ultimately we live and breathe in God and because of God. It may be hard to know when to stop fighting, and what kinds of medical technology to eschew; but the effort of discerning, and the risk even of erring, are not part of playing God so much as being human.

Families should carefully monitor what medical care is given. Doctors order a certain regimen, but they aren't around to make sure it's followed—and sometimes overworked nurses and orderlies overlook things. The best strategy in a hospital, especially for a long stay, is friendliness. You can bring fruit or cookies to the nurses, and take time to greet them by name. Then your questions are less likely to seem hostile. Occasionally, still, you have to be a pest.

But the most important attention will go to the person who is dying. Dr. Stephen Sheerin tells me that relatives and friends sometimes focus on the glittering technology that surrounds them in an intensive care unit, almost ignoring the person who is dying. Such distractions should be resisted, and your focus turned toward the person. What do you want to accomplish with him or her? Early on, before the dying person's strength is spent, there may be time for serious talk. If you have words of love and forgiveness, say them; you may not have another chance. This is a time for reconciliation and forgiveness, for shared grief and shared love. Don't put it off.

Talking with the Dying

Elisabeth Kubler-Ross and others have explored the process people go through in dealing with their own imminent death. Her components have become familiar: denial, anger, bargaining, depression and acceptance. These have often been misunderstood as stages that a person should follow in a more-or-less predictable sequence, with the one who reaches "acceptance" winning our admiration. In reality, people shift back and forth between the various components, and may experience several at once. Kubler-Ross's work has been enormously helpful in allowing us to recognize the commonness and normalcy of these reactions, so often a part of grieving.

Most people, nonetheless, find it hard to talk about these topics—about death, because it seems indecent, and about life after death, because it seems unreal. The dying is so physical, so grievous, that sometimes heaven seems (to visitors) like a frivolous, sentimental get-well card. Such it is not. And often dying people do not feel it as such. Many take life after death very seriously, and exert their curiosities to understand it, to wonder at it. Simone de Beauvoir reports that though, in Europe, the belief in life after death has declined, it seems to rise dramatically when people grow old. Perhaps this is because it seems more pertinent. It's perfectly natural and desirable to talk about death and the afterlife with someone who is dying.

Later, as they draw nearer to death, most people do not want a great deal of conversation. Often they lack energy to speak. But they often can hear, even when they cannot talk. Prayers, Scripture reading, music (particularly familiar hymns) are appropriate. The sense of touch outlasts sight; holding hands conveys your closeness and your continuing love.

The dying usually want, above all, not to be left alone, especially by those who love them. Yet Thomas Powers writes, "Doctors, nurses and even relatives tend to find good reasons to stay out of the dying patient's room. The pretense is that no one wants to 'disturb' the dying person while he is 'resting,' but nurses say they have seen too many clusters of relatives outside hospital rooms at the moment of death to consider it a coincidence." At the point of death, a person is not "resting up" for anything. He may as well spend his strength on those whom he loves.

"Grandpa got sick Saturday but we thought it was just a cold and did not call the doctor until Monday when we found he had viral pneumonia. I talked to [my sister] Ruth but we decided she should not come because he was much better Tuesday. I sat over there about 20 [hours] out of the 24 most days from Monday on, but did go to school for three hours Wednesday. When I got back he was okay, but Thursday he was worse and we sent for Ruth. It was storming and Continental cancelled their flights out of Denver but Frontier flew. Ruth got here by about 1:00 A.M. Friday. She stayed with him a while after 2:00 A.M. when I came home to get some sleep.

"[The next morning] he was very weak but fully conscious and knew us all and spoke words of love to all who came (and there were a constant stream of Manor [nursing home] workers who loved him). Ruth and I gave him his bed bath and he was so much better that I was embarrassed to have called Ruth, and put on my coat to go get my hair done.

"Then he began to have terrible breathing, so I took off my coat. We fought the phlegm, wiped out his mouth, and used a syringe and then finally the suction machine. But then he shut his mouth and had what looked to me like a massive hemorrhage in his forehead and stopped breathing. Ruth and I were on each side of him and we sang 'Safely Guarded' (very flat and crying), 'The Lord's My Shepherd,' and 'In the Land of Fadeless Day' (a great favorite of his). Ruth was able to say Jude 24 (his favorite all along) and several other verses he loved. I was crying too hard but we both held him and he began to breathe again. I prayed, 'Lord, don't let him be a vegetable,' and after about six long, slow breaths he stopped again.

"Ruth said, 'Daddy, you're changing,' because he had written her that in the Gaelic there is no word for human death (only animal and plant), only the word 'change.' I think he had one bad minute when he couldn't breathe and that was before the hemorrhage, and he was gone by 11:45 so he had 45 minutes of being really bad and 1 minute maybe 1 ½ minutes of pain. Not bad for 86 years and he never lost consciousness until the very end but loved us with his eyes and we held him close. Chase and Dr. Simpson came and the nurse stood with her arm around me. He didn't want to go to the hospital and how glad he will be to be in the presence of the King. He was a real soldier and I laid his plaid blanket over him as I would have laid a flag if I had had one, and left him."

from a letter my mother wrote me in Kenya,
after my grandfather's death

A Good Death

When a man or woman is old and, in biblical language, "full of years," death cannot seem the tragedy it seems when it takes a younger person. Death appears to rob the old ones of nothing; they have lived a full life, and families say good-bye, mingling tears and love. All my grandparents died in this way, except my father's father who died long before I was born. They had lived fully and well, and they were believers. As a child, as an adolescent and as an adult I received one consistent perception of their passing: sadness and solemnity and gratitude, as when you finish the last page of a great book or listen to the final strains of a great symphony.

Elisabeth Kubler-Ross and others have, in breaking the taboos of silence around death, helped us regain a more positive feeling about it, as something awesome and yet strangely familiar. Until she came, death was treated as a twentieth-century embarrassment and failure, particularly by hospitals and doctors. She has freed countless dying individuals and their families from the necessity of suffering in silence as they prepare for death. She has given us the psychological freedom to take death out of the hospital and into the home.

Yet in an odd sense her work has also tended to obscure death. This is very seldom noticed: since Kubler-Ross we have shifted our focus. When you attend a seminar on "death" nowadays, you will probably not talk of death at all, but human reactions to death. Death and its supernatural dimensions, which have been the concern of human beings since the beginning of time, will barely be mentioned. The discussion is on how it *feels* to approach death—not on what it means.

The feelings, however, float about in a vacuum unless we know what death actually is. It's not enough to identify what emotional stage people are in. In fact, that is essentially a sideshow, like identifying what the feelings of GIs were before they landed on the beach at Normandy. More important was: What is this fight all about? And who will win?

People who are dying want to know, and ought to know if they can, what death means for them. If they are to accept death—Kubler-Ross's fifth stage—what are they accepting? And should they? If death is the final insult to human pretensions, as many have thought, it might be better to take up Dylan Thomas's words: "Do not go gentle into that good night; rage, rage against the dying of the light."

What Is Death?

Very common today is the belief that we must accept death as biologically natural. There is more than a hint of Eastern philosophy here: accepting your place in the great flow of the universe, accepting yourself as a drop in the ocean of human life. Not many quite call us to *affirm* death. The attitude of acceptance is closer to resignation—submission to a benevolent nature, or at least to biological necessity.

Others would accept death because they believe it to be an illusion—a mere transfer point on the way to some happy after-death. Since people began reporting their near-death experiences, in which they saw a kindly light, or a loving Christ-figure at the end of a tunnel, a great many more people have gained faith in a benevolent existence beyond the grave. The spreading belief in reincarnation is usually presented equally optimistically. It ought not to be hard to accept death if you believe that there is no real death, that you go right on living but in a better way.

This is not the place to debate these interpretations of death. I want to make clear that the Christian tradition differs from them, however. For Christians, death is never merely natural, nor is it an illusion. Death and sin are unnatural and monstrous twins, since Adam's sin was at the origin of death. As Paul put it, "in Adam all died." This means that Adam's broken relationship with God was carried forward in every life; as surely as we were born, we alienate ourselves from God as Adam did, and as surely as we have sinned, we will die. "What a wretched man I am! Who will rescue me from this body of death?" wrote Paul (Rom. 7:24). For Paul, death was much more than the moment when a heart stops beating. Death was the process which destroyed the whole beloved person. Death begins at birth. It works throughout our lives, in our bodies and in our souls, until physical death puts its final seal on our destruction.

We were meant for something better. Death may not be an enemy of life as we experience it on earth, but it is an enemy of life as God intends it—full, unending, unhindered life with God and with others, life as God gave it when he first breathed it into human beings, and life as he offers it to all through the revived life of Jesus.

Keeping Calm While Facing an Enemy

But then, if death is an enemy, how can a Christian die as my grandfather did—"old and full of years"—with family around who are reasonably serene in the face of death? A Christian can accept death, but the acceptance does not mean he regards death as natural. A Christian can accept death because he accepts Jesus as his Savior from death. He lies down in faith that God will raise him up. He accepts the darkness because he knows he will be carried into the light.

Dying Christians are on the verge of seeing Jesus, at last. They will be changed, just from finally meeting Jesus. They will be made like him (1 John 3:2). Paul's words are powerful ones for the dying person to hear: "Neither death nor life, neither angels nor demons, neither the present nor the future, nor any powers, neither height nor depth, nor anything else in all creation, will be able to separate us from the love of God that is in Christ Jesus our Lord" (Rom. 8:38–39).

Our bodies will be made different, too. How so? We do not know. But old people need to know that their old, worn-out bodies will be renewed and changed, never to be worn down again. They will have no aches and pains, no falls or foot troubles. When the New Testament tells about the resurrection of our bodies, it doesn't mean to say that we will live with this same old biological entity. It means to tell us that *we* will come to life again, not some spiritual essence. We are physical people, and as such will live— but the physical will no longer limit us.

Finally, we will meet loved ones on the other side of death. Scripture is quiet about this, while dying people often find it the aspect of afterlife most attractive to ponder. Old people usually have dozens of loved ones—spouses, children, brothers, sisters, parents, friends—who have already died. They miss these people; they long to see them, and they usually can imagine seeing them more easily than they can imagine meeting Jesus, whom they have never seen. Indeed, it is a beautiful hope, though it would seem that the hope of seeing Jesus will, on that day, be far brighter.

All these great things come to the Christian after death, but not because of death. They come because of Jesus, victor over all destructive powers. He himself died and yet broke free from death; he forced a way out that others can follow. He is the triumphant Lord of death; he stands over the deathbed with a flaming sword, defying all powers, and ready to lead his children to his home. He is not merely the shining light at the end of a dark tunnel; by sheer authority he holds open the tunnel.

While death is an enemy, therefore, it also becomes the point of triumph. Like a poisonous snake whose fangs have been pulled, death remains malevolent and fearful. It will strike anyone. But the person struck need no longer die. "Where, O death, is your victory? Where, O death, is your sting?" (1 Cor. 15:55). Christians can accept death, not because it is natural, but because its unnaturalness has been swallowed by life.

Philippe Aries, in his fascinating history of European attitudes toward death, points out that one of the most visible, undeniable changes that occurred when Christianity spread throughout Europe was that people stopped fearing the dead. Always before, through centuries of Rome and Greece and other civilizations, dead bodies were buried far outside the town. The dead were a source of terror, until Christian faith transformed people's view. Then, the dead were buried around and even in the church; the cemetery became a meeting place, a market, a hub of activity.

But, says Aries, the terror of the dead has returned. He points out that in the eighteenth and nineteenth centuries the dead were again removed from our midst. "Rural cemeteries" were organized; people became afraid of dead bodies, and they placed them (however artistically) away from human activity. To Aries, as a cultural historian, this is one piece of evidence among many that death is feared today far more than during medieval times. He suggests that the use of medical technology on the dying maintains the fiction that death is an "accident of illness that must be brought under control." He suggests that the more recent therapeutic attitude toward death attempts to achieve the same anesthesia by other means. "Both attitudes, which are really very close, are responses to the uneasiness caused by the continued existence of death in a world that is eliminating suffering: moral suffering—hell and sin—in the nineteenth century; and physical suffering—pain and disease—in the twentieth (or twenty-first) century. Death should have disappeared along with disease, but it persists; it is not even any longer in retreat. Its persistence is a scandal."

Death is objectively fearful. In secular terms, it mocks our pretensions to significance, and in Christian insight, it is the last nail in a coffin of self-destruction we have been building since Adam. It cannot be dealt with by a psychological process alone. Our reaction to death is not the central problem; death itself is the problem. It destroys us. If our lives are to have any ultimate significance, death must be overturned, its power neutralized. So it has been. We triumph in this life through Christ, and the greatest triumph of faith comes at the end. This the dying should know.

Death offers the final phase of growing past 65. It eliminates, fully and absolutely, any possibility of triumphing by our own abilities. At death, the darkness is complete. There is only one hope: in God. Those who realize it, and put their faith in him during this last struggle, know all they need to know about growing.

Now I further saw, that betwixt them and the gate was a river; but there was no bridge to go over, and the river was very deep. At the sight, therefore, of this river, the pilgrims were much stunned; but the men that went with them said, "You must go through. . . ."

The pilgrims then, especially Christian, began to despond in his mind, and looked this way and that; but no way could be found by them by which they might escape the river. Then they asked the men if the waters were all of a depth. They said, "No"; yet they could not help them in that case; "for," said they, "you shall find it deeper or shallower as you believe in the King of the place."

Then they addressed themselves to the water; and, entering, Christian began to sink, and crying out to his good friend Hopeful, he said, "I sink in deep waters; the billows go over my head; all His waves go over me. Selah."

Then said the other, "Be of good cheer, my brother; I feel the bottom, and it is good." Then said Christian, "Ah! my friend, the sorrows of death have compassed me about; I shall not see the land that flows with milk and honey." And with that, a great darkness and horror fell upon Christian, so that he could not see before him. . . .

Hopeful, therefore, here had much ado to keep his brother's head above water; yea, sometimes he would be quite gone down, and then, ere a while, he would rise up again half dead. Hopeful would also endeavor to comfort him, saying, "Brother, I see the gate, and men standing by to receive us"; but Christian would answer, "It is you, it is you they wait for: you have been hopeful ever since I knew you." "And so have you," said he to Christian. "Ah, brother," said he, "surely, if I were right, He would now arise to help me; but for my sins He hath brought me into this snare, and hath left me. . . ."

Then I saw in my dream that Christian was in a muse awhile. To whom also Hopeful added these words, "Be of good cheer, Jesus Christ maketh thee whole." And with that, Christian brake out with a loud voice, "Oh, I see Him again; and He tells me, 'When thou passest through the waters, I will be with thee; and through the rivers, they shall not overflow thee.'" Then they both took courage; and the enemy was, after that, as still as a stone, until they were gone over. Christian, therefore, presently found ground to stand upon; and so it followed that the rest of the river was but shallow. Thus they got over.

from John Bunyan's *Pilgrim's Progress*

The Seventh Day:
Sabbath

THE SIX DAYS OF OLD AGE ARE FULL AND DE-manding. They certainly are not characterized, as a whole, by "taking it easy." But the six days end, and there is a seventh day: Sabbath, the day of rest.

Elders who die trusting in Jesus truly can rest. They rest not in the sense of ceasing activity. They rest in ending their restlessness. They find their niche. They rest in joy.

Their family, left behind, also rests. Many of them could not have sustained their efforts, physically and emotionally, much longer. Something had to break. It did. Death came, and they have entered a period of recuperation.

When I was a boy, my parents kept a fairly strict Sabbath. They took naps, and we children could read or play quietly. We were not allowed to listen to ball games, or watch TV. Sabbath wasn't kept religiously—that is, code violations weren't regarded as offenses against God. As my parents taught us, the day was a break for us, not for God. We needed the rest. I have a strong memory of spending drowsy Sunday afternoons bored and quiet, performing that most ritual task of reading the Sunday newspaper. It was not necessarily joyful to stop what we busily did all week, but it was restorative.

That is what is needed in the Seventh Day of aging, after a parent or friend has gone. You need to let it all sink in. You need to let your soul catch up with your body. You need time to process all that has gone before. If you have been through a bruising, drawn-out week of aging, this is a time when you can recapture the whole person whom you love, who affected your life, and who is gone. This is a time for honoring your parent.

Honoring Your Parents

The command to honor parents is positive—one of only two in the Ten Commandments. The command puts it so that we are not given a sin to avoid, but a virtue to aim for.

The root word in Hebrew is "weight." To honor your father and mother means to give them weight in the community. One does this primarily by living in a manner that gives them credit—by achieving great things, by living well, by demonstrating discipline and wisdom. You honor your parents by being the kind of person that makes a parent say proudly, "That's my kid."

One also gives parents weight by acting respectfully toward them. When a child cares for his elderly father and mother, when he steadies them and assists them, he is giving them honor.

After that is all over and the Seventh Day has come, you can honor them in your thoughts by recalling their lives. The last days of aging may have been a nightmare. The Seventh Day allows you to step back and see the whole life. Going through photo albums, reading old letters, sorting through possessions, sharing memories with siblings and other friends and relations—these are tasks of the Seventh Day that help you remember what was good and laugh at what was not so good. This is part of honoring your parents: honoring their memory.

Healing Memories

Old age is a frightening prospect in our times, no longer a distinction and a blessing, but rather a source of anxiety. It may be that "honoring your parents" has never been easy; it is certainly not today.

I spoke recently with a friend who has not visited his mother, who is in a nursing home with Alzheimer's disease, for four years. She doesn't recognize him and, he says, "I don't need those memories."

Yet we must all have memories, and seldom do we have only the memories we would choose to have. My friend will still have memories: of choosing not to see his mother. I think I would rather have the memories of seeing her, dreadful as those may be. But then, I do not know what it is like to have a mother with Alzheimer's disease, so I cannot be sure.

Regardless of which choice is best, either would undoubtedly leave some nightmarish memories. The Seventh Day is a time for healing those memories. It is a time for looking back on adversity and thanking God for his help. It is a time for confessing guilt (and guilt feelings) and allowing them to be healed. It is a time for restoring your relationship with God, who (you may feel) deserted or betrayed you in your time of need.

Why Old Age?

Why must we go through the week of aging, anyhow? What do we gain? Individuals may gain this or that, according to the particular experience they have. For all of us, though, honoring parents through the Seven Days of old age reaffirms and clarifies the kind of people we are. Old age sometimes puts us under stress, but the stress reveals the caliber of work that went into our making. When we honor our parents, we honor God. When we honor our parents, we honor ourselves.

At this point in America's history, we may be approaching a crisis for the elderly. Sheer numbers threaten to overwhelm us. If our record of care is far from perfect now, what will it become? We shall see, and what we see will say volumes about us as a people.

Simone de Beauvoir writes, "It is the meaning that men attribute to their life, it is their entire system of values that define the meaning and the value of old age. The reverse applies: by the way in which a society behaves toward its old people it uncovers the naked, and often carefully hidden, truth about its real principles and aims."

Later in her book on old age, having looked at how we behave toward old people, she returns to this theme: "Old age exposes the failure of our entire civilization. It is the whole man that must be re-made, it is the whole relationship between man and man that must be recast if we wish the old person's state to be acceptable. A man should not start his last years alone and empty-handed. . . . If he were not atomized from his childhood, shut away and isolated among other atoms, and if he shared in a collective life, as necessary and as much a matter of course as his own, then he would never experience banishment. Nowhere, and in no century, have these conditions obtained."

De Beauvoir was no believer, but Christians can share her radical assessment. We can see what a truly good old age would require. But there exists no such utopia, and never since Eden has there existed such a utopia. "It is the whole man that must be re-made, it is the whole relationship between man and man that must be recast. . . ." We can only be re-made, and our society recast, by the breaking into history of our Maker.

Christians say that this has begun. We say that God has marked our lives—marked them with the sign of the cross. If this is so, it is reasonable to ask that we see signs of it in the way we honor our elders, especially our parents. Old age is a part of God's creation that seems, to many, devoid of glory. It seems like a dreadful mistake, or at best a useless by-product of life, like the dried-up cob of an ear of corn. It is our task to see the glory in this period, to understand what God is doing through it, and to encourage those growing through it. The task is not easy, and sometimes we will inevitably be confused and unable to see any good in it. That is why we need the full week of old age, including the Seventh Day.

The Seventh Day, the Sabbath, is a day of rest, of reflection, of worship. It is a day to honor God for what he has done in us, and what he still must do. It is a day for renewing our vision. For he has said: "I am making everything new!"

EPILOGUE

MEMO TO MY FATHER-IN-LAW:

YOU SAT IN OUR KITCHEN AND, CHARACTER-
istically, got to the point. *"I read through the whole manuscript,"*
you said, *"and I kept expecting to find out how you are going
to take care of me. Did I miss something?"*

How could I answer that? I said that it seemed pretty clear
that you had enough money to stay in your home as long as you
could wish, and that we were going to do everything we could
to support you and love you and work out the logistics of care
in that home. We can't know the details yet. Just the outline.

But your question underscored for me the lesson I have learned
from researching this book, from reading about and talking to
scores of older people. The lesson is that old age is not a problem
to be solved. It is part of life to be experienced, for the elder
and for his family.

I started with the problem-solving mentality, wanting to know
all about finances and nursing homes and home health care. I
wanted to have the answers. Now I know a great deal—much

more than I have put into this book—and it does help, but it hasn't provided answers, not absolute answers.

It has instead provided a deeper appreciation and reverence for life past 65. In the years ahead, as you and Ozzie and my mom and dad grow older, we will certainly struggle. How exactly? I don't know. Yet I face that uncertainty with confidence, because I now know that growing does not stop at 65. Aging is not a problem to be solved. It is a gift from God, full of life and growth and joy for those who have the eyes to see. I want to see it with you.

FURTHER RESOURCES

Growing Past 65

De Beauvoir, Simone. *The Coming of Age*. Translated by Patrick O'Bryan. Putnam, 1972. A remarkable, pessimistic *tour de force* of the societal issues raised by old age. Stimulating.

Nouwen, Henri J.M. and Gaffney, Walter J. *Aging: The Fulfillment of Life*. Image Books, 1976. A thoughtful, encouraging Christian meditation on the meaning of old age.

The First Day: Freedom

Atchley, Robert C. *The Sociology of Retirement*. Schenkman Publishing Company, 1976. This book presents sociological research and is, therefore, fairly technical, but it does eliminate many myths about retirement.

The American Association of Retired Persons (AARP). Write to the AARP Program Resources Dept., 1909 K Street NW, Washington, D.C. 20049, and ask for the program schedule and the catalog of publications. The AARP sponsors an astonishing variety of programs nationwide, and has an excellent publications department, offering free pamphlets on dozens of subjects. Membership is $5 per year for seniors (less for multiple years) and is a good investment, but the publications are available to all.

The First Day Continued: Practical Matters

Crystal, Stephen. *America's Old Age Crisis: Public Policy and the Two Worlds of Aging*. Basic Books, 1982. An in-depth explanation of the financial differences made by governmental involvement.

"Information on Medicare and Health Insurance for Older People." A pamphlet offered free of charge by AARP. Write to AARP Fulfillment, 1909 K Street NW, Washington, D.C. 20049.

The Second Day: Beginnings of Reflection

Becker, Arthur H. *Ministry With Older Persons: A Guide for Clergy and Congregations*. Augsburg, 1986. While the focus of this book is on church ministry, the perspectives are broad enough to make it extremely useful for lay readers. This is the best book I have found on the spiritual dimensions of old age.

Bianchi, Eugene C. *Aging As a Spiritual Journey*. Crossroad, 1985. Some intriguing ideas are explored in this oft-cited book, which draws on perspectives from several religions.

Hateley, Barbara J. *Telling Your Story, Exploring Your Faith*. St. Louis, MO: CBP Press, 1985. A highly regarded guide for life review.

The Third Day: Losing a Spouse

"Housing Choices for Older Homeowners" (D12026), "Housing Options for Older Americans" (D12063), and "Your Home, Your Choice" (D12143) are free booklets available from AARP, 1909 K Street NW, Washington, D.C. 20049. The first covers home equity conversions and other financial options for homeowners; the second outlines housing options; and the third is a workbook for help in making decisions about where to live.

"On Being Alone" (D150) is a free booklet available from
     AARP. It is a guide for the newly widowed.

The Fourth Day: Role Reversal

Otten, Jane and Shelley, Florence D. *When Your Parents Grow
     Old.* Funk & Wagnalls, 1976. A very practical "how-
     to" guide aimed at caregivers.

The Fifth Day: Dependency

Gillies, John. *A Guide to Caring for and Coping with Aging
     Parents.* Thomas Nelson, 1981. An extremely practical
     and sensitive guide, which draws extensively on Gillies'
     personal experiences with his mother and father-in-
     law. It's particularly helpful for dealing with a highly
     dependent parent.

Mace, Nancy L. and Rabins, Peter V. *The 36-Hour Day: A
     Family Guide to Caring for Persons with Alzheimer's Dis-
     ease, Related Dementing Illnesses and Memory Loss in
     Later Life.* Johns Hopkins. The "Bible" for the families
     of Alzheimer's victims.

"Q & A: Alzheimer's Disease." An AARP pamphlet (D661),
     available free of charge from AARP Fulfillment, 1909
     K Street NW, Washington, D.C. 20049.

The Sixth Day: Saying Good-bye

Aries, Philippe. *The Hour of Our Death.* Translated by Helen
     Weaver. Alfred A. Knopf, 1981. The landmark his-
     torical study of attitudes toward death. Long, heavy,
     and highly thought-provoking.

Kubler-Ross, Elisabeth. *On Death and Dying.* Macmillan, 1970.
     A classic that continues to be very helpful.

Tim Stafford is the editor of Campus Life Books. He graduated from Stanford University with a Bachelor of Arts degree in Creative Writing and has authored several books.